MW00769824

PRAISE FOR PROPHEC

I've pastored "prophetic" churches for over 25 years. That means that we have openly encouraged the corporate and individual hearing of God's voice. We've seen the good, the bad, and the ugly. Most of the challenges arise out of not understanding the"rules of engagement." When people have a clear mandate with solid training and coaching, fruit abounds.

Graham Cooke has a solid history as a writer, trainer, and activator of the prophetic. This book is a training tool for safely lifting your church into becoming a prophetic voice for the kingdom, in and out of the church context. I recommend Graham's resources for the further equipping of the Lord's church. The prophetic needs to be monitored and mentored. Let Graham be your coach into the shifting of the prophetic from a curse to a blessing!

Steve Witt
President, Edify Ministries International

It is a joy for me to highly commend Graham's latest book, *Prophecy & Responsibility*. As a local church pastor, and a member of the Canadian Prophetic Council, this book is long overdue for those of us who pastor, prophesy, and receive prophecy.

Graham is a dear friend who has salted our congregation and city leadership many times with his wisdom, wit, and the wonder of how God continues to speak. He challenges us to honestly listen to all God is saying — thus the need for process and protocol.

You will find yourself centered in the Word of God that reminds us that prophecy is something we should earnestly desire. It is also about edification, exhortation, and comfort that flows out of our love for God and His people.

He teaches three important protocols that make prophets and prophecy healthier and more effective:

1. Guidelines for handling prophecy.
2. Evaluating the prophetic word.
3. Handling wrong prophecy.

I encourage you to read *Prophecy & Responsibility* as a manual for prophetic maturity. Graham guides us through prophetic exercises on the fruit of the Spirit, case studies, and journal assignments that lead us to a 21st century version of a healthy prophetic church.

Dr. Barry P. Boucher (Rev.)
Senior Pastor, The Life Centre Ottawa, Canada

Thank the Lord for Graham Cooke's latest book on prophetic ministry. Revelation has seldom been a problem in the Church but the governance of the gift has not always been well handled. Graham gives us real and practical help on how to interpret and implement prophetic words. This will be an invaluable tool for all in church leadership and I strongly recommend it.

Paul Reid
Senior Pastor, Christian Fellowship Church Belfast, Ireland

This unique book is a"must read"for prophetic people, church leaders, and those seeking to understand more of God's ways in their own lives and generation. It is typical of Graham's inspired wisdom and insight which draw on decades of his own journey and experience in training and equipping prophetic people in many nations. If there is a handbook for prophetic foundation and practical protocol, this is probably it (coupled with *Developing Your Prophetic Gifting* — one of his previous writings)! Apart from being a work of stature, it expresses the heart of a man who knows the love and kindness of God, intimately...

Peter Stott

This book is packed with wisdom from the front lines of battle. Every page emanates Graham Cooke's deep passion to see a mature expression of the gift of prophecy emerge in the church. With powerful illustrations Graham walks us through the minefield of the mishandling of the gift of prophecy. And what a minefield it is! Graham's stature as a senior prophetic teacher continues to grow as he teaches us, through personal experience, how to discern between the polluted streams and the pure living water. Graham is a focused and progressive thinker. As I read this book I kept sensing that he is answering questions that many of us have not yet asked in our journey into the prophetic. This book is a quantum leap forward in the art of ministering prophetically with maturity, accountability, and wisdom. As the pastor of a prophetic community I am personally thankful to Graham for yet another indispensable volume and for his obedience to the Spirit in leaving this invaluable paper trail.

Phil Mason
Senior Leader, New Earth Tribe Byron Bay, Australia

From a pastoral viewpoint, Graham's newest book, *Prophecy & Responsibility,* cannot be published soon enough! It is rich with wisdom and experiential knowledge. It answers the questions people are asking about the prophetic. I've had the privilege of knowing Graham since 1995,and his words — both spoken and written — have mentored me through the years. Like so many of his other books, trying to highlight key thoughts is an exercise in futility — you might as well just highlight whole pages at a time! And like so many of his other books, this one can be read over and over again without exhausting the revelation it contains.

The foundational truths expressed are saturated with kindness and humility, and they provide a practical framework for cultivating healthy and diverse expressions of prophetic ministry. In the heart of this book, Graham writes,"The world today desperately needs a prophetic church." *Prophecy & Responsibility* is a hands on resource tool to help bring this into reality. I wholeheartedly recommend this book. Read it, experience it, and as Graham so often says, "Enjoy the journey."

David Danielson
Pastor, Impact Christian Fellowship, Kerrville, Texas

Graham Cooke hits the mark again!! His practical teaching in *Prophecy & Responsibility* will help churches and individuals in their prophetic ministry. We use all his books in our prophetic schools in the Northwest and the maturing of those being trained by his teaching is very evident. Graham's realness, humor, transparency, spirituality, Biblical accuracy, and intimacy with God shine through brilliantly.

This book calls individuals and leaders into accountability to the Lord and one another. This is a must read. This is a great book for all interested in prophetic ministry. Keep it up Graham! We love you and need you!

Dan Hammer
Sonrise Chapel, Everett, Washington

For 14 years now I've seen Graham's teachings shape my life and the lives of many other individuals and churches. As a pastor, I don't know of anyone who brings the wealth of deep revelation and at the same time amazingly practical application of the prophetic that Graham brings forth. His insights into the operation of the prophetic in the church are incredibly liberating, refreshing, and unifying. The treasures contained in this book will not only inspire you to go deeper in the greatest adventure of knowing God, they will empower you to reveal His kindness to the world.

Steve Fish
Senior Pastor, James Avenue Church Fort Worth, Texas

Through many years my friend, Graham Cooke, has allowed the Trinity to shape him into the unique vessel that he has become. He is a man who knows God, appreciates the breadth of His kingdom, loves the yet imperfect church of Jesus in her various and colorful forms, is a passionate practitioner of the knowledge he has gained, and is a humble and courageous explorer into the things of God yet to be heard and known. *Prophecy & Responsibility* is another very important contribution from Graham's heart and experience to the Body of Christ that will help round us out to express more fully the treasure that is the life of Jesus that the Father has invested in us — His deeply loved jars of clay.

Michael Sullivant
Author and Pastor, Metro Christian Fellowship Kansas City, Missouri

Graham Cooke is one of the rarest commodities in the Body of Christ – he is a prophet who has chosen relationships above personal gifting. This Kingdom priority qualifies him to write *Prophecy & Responsibility*. These pages overflow with wisdom and insights that cannot be found in the writings of a theorist. They were born in community. As a pastor I recommend this book because it is safe. As a revivalist I recommend it because it provokes one to a life of risk. And it is extremely rare to find both elements in one book.

Bill Johnson
Author of *When Heaven Invades Earth*

My friendship with Graham is both enjoyable and life changing. In his latest book *Prophecy & Responsibility,* I see a giant leap forward in the practice of prophecy. A prophetic word, given with understanding and grace, can spur a church, community or individual into spiritual breakthrough. But given incorrectly, a word can actually hinder what Holy Spirit wants to do. Graham Cooke's credibility, experience, and integrity give him the ability to speak into how Holy Spirit, churches, leaders and prophets can advance the Kingdom together.

Jesse Padgett
Preacher/hot-rod builder/ventriloquist/banjo player/comedian… friend

Graham Cooke's new book, *Prophecy & Responsibility,* is destined to be one of the most practical tools the Holy Spirit will use to enrich and deepen the lives of many who desire to begin to move or move more powerfully in the gift of prophecy. I love the way the book is structured and the very practical applications and readings at the end of the chapters. The sidebars telling the stories of great people in the Kingdom of God who moved in prophecy after the apostolic age is a great encouragement to us who do believe God still speaks to his church.

I am excited about this second of six books in this series that Graham will write. I will encourage its reading by the students at our Global School of Missions, Church Planting, and Supernatural Ministry. I wish I could have had this book to read when I was younger. I truly believe that some of the mistakes I have made as a leader could have been avoided if I had known the contents of *Prophecy & Responsibility*. Many pains in the lives of my parishioners, friends, my wife and I could have been avoided by the application of the wisdom of this book.

I believe every leadership team of every church should study this book and discuss how their church will develop its own prophetic protocol. From 1994–1998 my ministry and church co-sponsored Graham and several other prophets at our annual prophetic conference. During those five years, no teaching tapes sold more than Graham's. In addition, he was used of God more than once in a prophetic consultant role to bring peace to a troubled time in my last pastorate. Now, the basis for this wisdom and the proper way to allow the prophetic to strengthen people is made clear in *Prophecy & Responsibility*. If I were to go into details regarding all the things that impressed me with the book, space would not allow it to be an endorsement; it would become its own chapter. I consider Graham Cooke one of the most respected prophetic persons I know who not only has a prophetic gift, but who is in the office of the prophet. It will be hard to find a more practical book to help you grow in either giving or pastoring prophecy.

Graham has walked through many rough seasons in his life and I am proud to watch him live out his life with great integrity and faithfulness to the author of all prophecy. Graham has been faithful to continue to bear the testimony of Jesus which is the spirit of prophecy.

Randy Clark
Global Awakening, Harrisburg, Pennsylvania

Prophecy & Responsibility is relevant for our day. The explosion of prophetic ministry among God's people is upon us now! Graham's years of experience and insight into this ministry will accelerate God's purposes in the release of the prophetic, as well as provide healthy pathways, principles, and cautions that could save us years in its development. A great tool for prophets, leaders, as well as the Body of Christ at large!

Rodney Odom
Senior Leader, Grace Church High Point, North Carolina

PROPHECY & RESPONSIBILITY

BY GRAHAM COOKE

GUIDELINES FOR HANDLING PROPHECY

EVALUATING THE PROPHETIC WORD

WHAT TO DO WITH WRONG PROPHECY

www.BrilliantBookHouse.com

Prophecy & Responsibility is the second of six books in the *Prophetic Equipping* Series.

Brilliant Book House LLC
865 Cotting Ln, Ste C
Vacaville, California USA 95688
www.brilliantbookhouse.com

© 2009 by Graham Cooke

All rights reserved. No part of this book may be reproduced, stored in a retrieval system, or transmitted in any form or by any means – electronic, mechanical, photocopy, recording, or otherwise – without prior written permission of the copyright owner and publisher, except by a reviewer who wishes to quote brief passages in connection with a review for inclusion in a magazine, newspaper or broadcast.

Unless otherwise indicated, all Scripture quotations are taken from The Holy Bible, NEW AMERICAN STANDARD BIBLE. Copyright © 1960, 1962, 1963, 1971, 1972, 1973, 1975, 1977, 1995 by The Lockman Foundation. Used by permission.

Requests for information should be addressed to:

Graham Cooke

office@myemerginglight.com

ISBN 978-1-934771-15-0

Printed in the United States of America.

Cover designed by Matt Nowicki

DEDICATION

I dedicate this book to Mark and Sophie Marie Patten, my son-in-law and daughter, and also to their first child, Evelyn Rose, born during the writing of this book. I've watched you guys following after something bigger, bolder, and better. I love you both and am proud and grateful to share your journey.

ACKNOWLEDGMENTS

To all pastors everywhere who value the prophetic and work to make it pure and powerful. Thank you for understanding that it's the process that is provoked by prophecy that makes us become the people that God is looking for to fulfill His purpose.

When we let go of process, we let go of the one single means of determining our character, identity, and destiny.

To the community of my friends who love process and the inner development of God's workings through everyday life.

To all prophets who have not given up on church but who have used betrayal and rejection properly. That is, allowed it to develop a greater passion for what God has most set His heart on. Blessed are you. May God use you more powerfully in the preparation of His Bride.

To those who became embittered and judgmental at the treatment you received. It's not too late to grow up, stand up, and take the place that God has been holding open for you. The dead are never betrayed. They're just dead.

If you are still wounded, you did not die. The cross had no effect on your carnality. It's time to put that right. May you find the life that has always been present in Christ Jesus and live that life in the fullness that the Father intended.

Contents

INVOCATION

Everything about You, Father, we love. We love Your ways, we love Your heart for us, and we love the fact that You're consistent in everything. Father, we are learning to be more amazed by You. Thank You for this journey that we're on, a journey right into Your very heartbeat.

Help us to discover the truth that You will not rest until we see You as You want to be seen. Open the eyes of our hearts, our inner man, the eyes of our understanding. Let us behold You in new ways in this season of our lives. Let us discover that You are more for us than anything we ever thought previously. Let us understand something of the majesty and the greatness of Your affection for us.

Holy Spirit, we revere and bless You for Your ministry to us, and for making real the things of Christ. We bless You in Your ministry. Help us to be more disciplined, more open, and more God-conscious, so that we may respectfully walk with You. Let us not grieve You in any way.

Help us to rest in the revelation that You bring to our hearts about Your nature. Thank You for Your presence with us. Please come and do what You do best: teach us, inspire us, show us the Father, reveal the Son to us, and touch our hearts. If there is anything in our lives that needs a positive adjustment, we pray that You would make it today.

Amen.

INTRODUCTION

"It will come about after this that I will pour out My Spirit on all mankind; And your sons and daughters will prophesy, your old men will dream dreams, your young men will see visions. Even on the male and female servants I will pour out My Spirit in those days" (Joel 2:28–29)

THE WORLD CHANGED THE DAY the Holy Spirit fell on Jesus' remaining disciples in that famed upper room in Jerusalem. The Spirit of God, reserved in the Old Testament for a select few, had now been placed on anyone who sought and loved Christ. With that outpouring came the gifts of the Spirit. While once only a few could prophesy, suddenly everyone could.

I have been in the prophetic ministry since 1974. I began prophesying the year before. That's more than thirty years of sharing the love God has placed in my heart. Amazingly, I'm still learning — and I never want to stop. Every year, I understand something new about God and His ways. He never ceases to intrigue me.

More than a decade ago, my book, *Developing Your Prophetic Gifting,* was first published. It has been a greater success than I could have ever imagined. Hundreds of thousands of copies have been sold. But I've come a long way in the years since I wrote that first manuscript. For one thing, I have taught countless prophetic schools during that time. As I work with students and emerging prophetic voices, I have had my own gift shaped and honed. "Iron sharpens iron, so one man sharpens another," as it says in Proverbs 27:17. The people I have met have pushed me further into the things of the prophetic. They have challenged me to find fresh ways of equipping, explaining, and encouraging.

For several months, I have felt the Lord prompt me to expand *Developing Your Prophetic Gifting,* adding the material I have taught in my schools over the past ten years. This book is the second of six manuals that will more fully equip people longing to speak the words of God to those around them.

Together, we will study the practical elements of hearing God, of moving in the Spirit, of knowing God's nature, and of representing His heart to someone else. We will learn how to be grounded in the love, grace, and rhythm of God. It is my prayer that these books will give you something fresh about who God wants to be for you. As you read the principles and illustrations within, I pray that you will be excited and inspired to venture further into what God has for you.

Prophecy comes when we have a burden to encourage and bless the people around us. There is no magic formula to prophesying; it all depends on our love for God. When we love Him fully, that love should spill over onto the people around us. Prophecy is simply encouraging, exhorting, and comforting people by tuning them into what God has for them. In every church in the world, there are people who need that life-giving word from God. These aren't just the individuals who are obviously struggling; some appear to have everything together. But God knows what's really going on.

Everyone could benefit from a prophetic word, even those for whom everything is soaring. I love to prophesy over people who are doing really well. If we can target those people and increase their faith at a critical time, they can fly even higher in the things of the Spirit.

Prophecy that is edifying and comforting will encourage us to look into the heart of God so that we see ourselves in His image. When we build on that flow of encouragement we can see directive prophecy propelling us into places of faith, vision, power, and anointing in the service of the King. The two together produces a company of people who are strong in the Lord and ready to do exploits (Daniel 11:32 KJV). Blessing and encouragement stir up anointing. The more of this kind of prophecy we can have in church, the less we will need intensive, time-consuming pastoral care. People will actually be touched by God and come into the things of the Spirit themselves. Individuals will realize that, yes, they are loved personally by God. That kind of revelation will stoke up their faith in ways a counseling session never could.

I know I need that kind of encouragement every day from the Holy Spirit. I can't remember the last time I asked Him to encourage me and He didn't. He may not speak it out immediately, but He always meets me at the point of my greatest need. That's just who the Holy Spirit is, and what He loves to do.

This book can help you go further in the prophetic than you have ever hoped. After all, "*things which eye has not seen and ear has not heard, and which have not entered the heart of man, all that God has prepared for those who love Him.*" (1 Corinthians 2:9)

Prophecy and Responsibility is divided into three chapters: *Guidelines for Handling Prophecy, Evaluating the Prophetic Word,* and *Handling Wrong Prophecy*. These chapters are not meant to be read in a day or a week; instead, I encourage you to take your time going through each, reading them until you understand the themes and thoughts they contain. Furthermore, don't neglect the exercises, case studies, and Bible readings included at the end of each chapter — they are valuable practice tools which will take the lessons taught and put them into practice in your life. Throughout this book, I have added some exercises on the nine characteristics of the fruit of the Spirit listed in Galatians 5. These exercises are meant to stretch and grow you to become more like Jesus.

Blessings on your journey into the prophetic!

Graham Cooke.

MODULE ONE

GUIDELINES FOR HANDLING PROPHECY

MODULE ONE

Guidelines For Handling Prophecy

WHAT YOU WILL LEARN IN THIS SEGMENT:

- God is deliberately vague to encourage us to explore.
- The difference between inspiration and revelatory prophecy.
- The importance of spiritual stimulation above soulish sentimentality.
- All prophecy provokes questions.
- Questions precipitate growth.
- How to move in encouragement and blessing as a lifestyle.
- Availability is the key to sensitivity in the Spirit.
- All revelatory prophecy is crafted, planned, and rehearsed.
- The difference between the influence of spontaneous prophecy and the authority and weight of revelatory words.
- The different elements of revelatory prophecy.
- How to work with 'present' and 'future' people.
- The importance of tension and paradox in the church.
- How to develop the proper methodology for directional prophecy.
- Guaranteeing the presence of God.
- Earning the right to speak and to prophesy.
- Working with leaders in partnership.

MODULE ONE

Guidelines For Handling Prophecy

WHAT YOU WILL LEARN IN THIS SEGMENT:

- The gap between the ideal and the actual and how to operate from that place.
- The meaning and the purpose of frustration.
- Weighing directional words before public delivery.
- Boundaries that are set by the Holy Spirit cannot quench Him.
- How to process prophecy to a place of ownership.
- How to deliver revelatory prophecy and fulfill the objective.
- Delivering difficult words and edifying the people.
- Proclamation is a key that unlocks hearts to God's identity for them.
- Learn how ministries can interact together.
- Principles of interpretation.
- The shallow end of living by faith.
- Applying the prophetic.
- Elements involved in the process of application.
- Provoking your own accountable lifestyle.
- The difference between preference and prejudice.
- Beware of the gulf between character and ministry.
- When public ministry is denied, private practice in the throne room is essential.

MODULE ONE

Guidelines For Handling Prophecy

HUMAN BEINGS LOVE CLARITY. We have been taught since birth to see and understand every detail and nuance of the things around us. We want to know every step of the journey. We prefer trips where every landmark, every turn, and every sign is clearly spelled out for us.

God isn't like that. Sometimes, He deliberately operates in vagueness. He is vague for a reason: He wants us to explore the possibility contained in His mysteriousness. In 1 Corinthians 12:4–6, the apostle Paul wrote of the variety of ways in which God interacts with His children: *"Now there are varieties of gifts, but the same Spirit. And there are varieties of ministries, and the same Lord. There are varieties of effects, but the same God who works all things in all persons."* God wants us to explore and discover His diversity and the different ways in which we perceive and relate to Him.

What if God had simply set out a checklist of the type of ministries He endorsed? What if 1 Corinthians 12:4–6 listed five types of prophetic ministry, five types of pastoral ministry, and five types of apostolic ministry? The church would simply have set those words in concrete and clung to them no matter what. Anyone or anything that didn't fit within God's checklist would be thrown out. Ministry would become homogenous, as everyone tried to be the same thing. The kingdom of God, once teeming with life and diversity, would become boring and sterile.

The Father's vagueness is our permission to explore

God wants us to explore our relationship with Him. He wants us to discover new things in the spirit. He wants us to ask the Holy Spirit questions about who He is, what He loves to do, and how He works. When He doesn't tell us something specific, He has a twinkle in His eye and a smile on His face because He knows He will soon have the joy of unfolding His plan with us.

He is deliberately vague so that He can entice us into exploration and discovery. He is always bigger than our experience of Him. His will for us is so huge only faith may discover it. His dreams for us are so big only a creative imagination may access it. The Holy Spirit increases our experience constantly, pulling us into a greater place of personal trust and outrageous faith and teaching us to move beyond mere logic and reason to a place where we can dwell in the bigness of God's calling and not be minimized or disenfranchised by our obvious humanity!

Prophecy isn't a perfect science, but while a static, scientific formula cannot be applied to it, there are certain trends and precedents that God usually operates through. These guidelines to handling prophecy aren't immutable and inviolable laws, however, using them will keep the prophetic minister accountable, humble, safe, and strong. They flow out of my thirty years of experience in prophetic ministry; many of them were learned through mistakes and trial and error. While we are all different in how we minister, as Paul said, we all want to serve the same God.

Inspirational Prophecy

Two types of prophecy exist: inspirational and revelatory prophecy. Every believer is able to prophesy on an inspirational level, especially in times of worship, because we have all been filled with the Spirit of God. In 1 Corinthians 14:1–5, Paul outlined his thoughts on prophecy.

> *Pursue love, yet desire earnestly spiritual gifts, but especially that you may prophesy. For one who speaks in a tongue does not speak to men but to God; for no one understands, but in his spirit he speaks mysteries. But one who prophesies speaks to men for edification and exhortation and consolation. One who speaks in a tongue edifies himself; but one who prophesies edifies the church. Now I wish that you all spoke in tongues, but even more that you would prophesy; and greater is one who prophesies than one who speaks in tongues, unless he interprets, so that the church may receive edifying.*

> *The Father's majesty can easily handle our humanity*

I believe it is possible for every child of God to prophesy at least once in his life because the Holy Spirit that fills us is inherently prophetic. The Spirit is visionary; He sees things in, around, and through us. He wants to link our present to our future. However, while everyone has the capacity to prophesy, not all are prophets. There is a world of difference between moving in the gift, moving in the ministry, and moving in the office of a prophet. They are three different developmental stages.

We can all bring edification, exhortation, and comfort. Inspirational prophecy refreshes people by injecting encouragement into their lives. It comforts them when they are in pain, it exhorts people to carry on following God, and it motivates their spirits to worship. This type of prophecy releases the joy of the

Lord, brings peace into someone's life, causes faith to rise, and births reverence for God. In short, it breeds the fruit of the Spirit listed in Galatians 5:22–23: "*But the fruit of the Spirit is love, joy, peace, patience, kindness, goodness, faithfulness, gentleness, self-control.*" All of these things happen in inspirational prophecy.

When we are developing in the prophetic gift, we need to run everything by someone else for a season. This is about teaching us accountability and healthy prophetic habits, not control. In my church, we don't believe in policing the prophetic, we believe in effectively pastoring it. We want to help develop prophets by asking them honest questions like, "How should this be delivered? Is this really what God wants to say?" As we nurture and develop their gift, they enter more and more freedom. Eventually, they get to a place in inspirational prophecy where we release them from having to check everything by one of us.

Inspirational prophecy is fairly innocuous. It shouldn't offend people and is often couched within a prayer for someone. At this level, people, especially beginners, find it difficult to distinguish between spiritual stimulation and soulish sentimentality. This can have a negative effect on congregations and meetings. Generally speaking, too much inspirational prophecy in a meeting is not useful, as it tends to take over. With so much inspiration happening, people can get used to it, close their ears to it, and fail to respond to either form of prophecy.

God speaks to us prophetically because He wants to do something in our lives. In order for Him to do what He says He will do, He needs some form of response from us. Whenever we have prophetic words spoken into our lives or into church meetings, there needs to be some kind of response. One of the major elements of the gifting, particularly in leaders, is how to interpret that response and answer the questions, "What does this mean?" and "What should we be doing?" (Acts 2). It is a skill and gift we need to develop in the church. Often the prophetic person may have done everything right, but the insecurity and inadequacy of the leadership can kill any response to the word. Prophecy can sometimes be unsettling because it can lead to repentance, change, and new direction. Responsive leaders understand that shift of the Holy Spirit and build a place for people to join it.

The root of inspirational prophecy is encouragement and blessing. We love the people around us enough to ask God questions about them. My friends tease me for being so incurably intentional with the Lord. I just love to know what He is doing in the people around me. I love walking into church Sunday morning, looking around, and thinking, "God, I love this place. I love these people." In my church, I know the tragedies and triumphs these people have walked through. I know their successes and failures, their gifts and difficulties. I feel a great kinship with them, and love to worship God with them. It bothers me when I see people standing at the back of a church with their arms folded and spirits shut down. Part of me wants to shake them up, so I ask God to show me what He is working on in them. "What are You up to, Lord?" I wonder. "Is there anything You want me to say or share?" My affection for other Christians leads me to want to see them blessed and encouraged.

I don't understand how anyone who loves God can be unimpressed by Him. The good news of the gospel is so good that we should be constantly pinching ourselves. What if the gospel is so good it's almost too good to be true? What if it is so amazing that it could border on fantasy? Instead of settling for something so much less than what Jesus died for, God wants to raise our sights to understand the power, wonder, brilliance, majesty, and awesomeness of His gospel. The chief element of being a servant of God is availability. We can be open to hearing from Him everywhere. Sitting in Starbucks, sipping a nonfat, no-whip caramel macchiato, we can be asking God about the people around us: "Is there anyone You want to connect with, Lord?" On an airplane, 35,000 feet above the earth, we can ask Him if there is anything He wants to say to the individual next to us. Stuck in traffic, we can ask God for a prophetic word for the person in the car ahead of us.

Availability is the key to sensitivity

We should always strive to become more God-conscious of the world around us. When we try to see the world as He does, we can spread more of His influence because we are readily available for whatever He wants to do.

Revelatory Prophecy

While inspirational prophecy is an important part of church life, revelatory prophecy is far deeper. Revelatory prophecy isn't spontaneous. It's often crafted, it's usually planned, it's generally rehearsed, and it's always prayed through before being given. Revelatory prophecy is simply too directive to be shared lightly.

A revelatory prophecy can include the following:

Words of Correction

We have not walked this way before. Our lives with the Lord are a constant learning experience. Usually when we do something for the first time, we learn how not to do it! Loving correction is a vital part of growth. It's always about the learning.

Real discipleship must be centered on providing loving essential feedback. Correction is about learning, not punishment. It should be joyful, caring, exciting, and meaningful. The attitude and persona that we take into a situation guarantees what we will take out of it!

Good leaders make correction a pleasure, a joy. Correction that comes via the prophetic carries the approachable heart of the Father. Wisdom is easy to entreat. It sets people free to learn and to become better for the experience. "*But the wisdom from above is first pure, then peaceable, gentle, reasonable, full of mercy and good fruits, unwavering, without hypocrisy. And the seed whose fruit is righteousness is sown in peace by those who make peace*" (James 3:17–18).

Godly wisdom seeks the blessing and release of the individual. It forms character in people because it is locked into the heart of God. The Father loves to see His people as He sees Jesus. When wisdom is released the presence of God unfolds as a cloak covering us with the attributes of His own nature. Purity, peace, gentleness, mercy, and righteousness flow towards the one being discipled in the character of God. We are not changed by changing our behaviors. We see who we really are in Christ and we behave accordingly. Wisdom releases identity.

Words of Direction, Opening Up Something New

Life is a journey and directions are important. We are all used to mapping out road trips — getting the best available maps, Triple A guidance, listening to the weather station and the latest traffic information. It's good to know stuff that will help you on the journey.

Prophecy can provide up-to-the-minute spiritual intelligence regarding the road ahead. "*Your ears will hear a word behind you, 'This is the way, walk in it,' whenever you turn to the right or to the left.*" (Isaiah 30:21)

God loves guidance. On every journey there is the seen and the unseen that accompany us on our travels. In relationship with the Father, we learn His ways and come to the place of understanding and interpreting His heart and mind. Prophecy tells us of the unforeseen and provides tactics and strategies to aid us on the road of life.

Some prophetic words will not make sense to us in the moment they are delivered. We must keep them close and pray through them often, asking God for wisdom. Many a time I have been saved in a part of my journey by a word previously given that had no connection with my then present but made every sense in my future.

Praying it through made me conscious of God somewhere on the road ahead watching over me and working for my good. The Holy Spirit prepares the way of the Lord in this manner. He helps us to live present–future and with a more keen awareness of cooperating with our destiny.

Words of Warning That May Require Repentance, a Change of Heart, a Change of Lifestyle, or a Change of Attitude

For a whole variety of reasons, words of warning are extremely important and can aid us considerably in our walk in the Spirit. First, we may be about to make decisions that are wrong for us and we need to be rescued and redirected.

Second, there are unscrupulous people who have personal agendas in our lives for their own satisfaction. I have met many such people, full of promises and offering all kinds of help and support, professing that God has sent them to help me. Over the years my experience has been that less than 10 percent of those have been genuine. Lots have been misguided, more have been opportunistic, and some have been sinister. How do I navigate my way through this myriad of human support without becoming cynical, bitter, wary, or suspicious?

I value my purity. I want to keep my innocence. I would rather be naïve than cynical; that's my choice. I need protecting. That's what a word of warning does for me. It protects my purity and my innocence. It protects my heart and my life from taking wrong turns and making wrong decisions.

Third, we live our lives in a war zone. We are caught up in a battle between darkness and light. Any soldier will inform you that advance intelligence is extremely valuable in a confrontation. Warnings protect us from the evil one.

Some warnings may necessitate repentance and readjustment on our part. The Father loves to watch over us and keep us from harm. Words of warning should be in line with God's passion to keep us close to His heart. He is our Keeper and He uses spiritual gifts to guide us through circumstances when we have not heard His whole counsel.

A word of warning can often be the Lord's last real attempt to keep us on track or restore us to the right path.

Words Highlighting a Way Forward, Defining a Faith or Prayer Agenda

God is always previous. I love the way He thinks about our lives. He is so present–future in how He perceives, thinks, and speaks. As befitting One who knows the end from the beginning, He does not want us running around being ignorant of His plan and purpose. He loves and needs us to see the way ahead and walk in a more purposeful manner.

New and future words give us a compass heading on life that enables us to pray more effectively and make the most of opportunities that the Father has created for our favor and blessing. He is wonderfully intentional toward us. He loves to speak things to us and over us that we then get to speak back to Him in faith, prayer, and confession.

In the Spirit we declare what God proclaims over us. We receive His agenda for our enlargement. Prophecy is a marvelous gift in that regard.

Revelatory words carry a different level of power and anointing. The words are more substantial. They are a catalyst for change. They have an inherent dynamic that if used wrongly or misunderstood may cause damage. They are more risky to use but carry incredible intentional power to divinely accelerate the lives of God's people. Revelatory prophecy can move people forward five years in twelve months. They carry a quickening spirit that must be understood. A greater partnership with the Holy Spirit and church leadership is required by the one prophesying.

The difference in depth between inspirational and revelatory prophecy is astounding. Inspirational words are given to get us into the presence of God.

Revelatory words prepare us for life, circumstances, events, and what God wants to do. They contain a challenge within them. God doesn't speak for novelty's sake. He speaks in order to create something, change something, overturn something, rule over something, or reward something. In Genesis 1:3: "*Then God said, 'Let there be light'; and there was light.*" Light was created by four of God's words. In Acts 10:15, God overturned an entire religious system by telling Peter, "*What God has cleansed, no longer consider unholy.*" In Luke 3:22, God honored Jesus after His baptism: "*You are My beloved Son, in You I am well pleased.*" Revelatory words more closely capture the creative nature of God than inspirational prophecy.

> *A true prophet is a brother, a friend, and a provocation*

Inspirational prophecy isn't going to hurt anyone — it just doesn't strike at that deep a level. The worst that can happen is that someone is given a blessing in the wrong area of his or her life. No one is likely to complain about that. But revelatory words can actually cause damage when the timing is wrong or when we miss them. As I have traveled around the world in the past thirty years, I have dealt with a lot of people who have been damaged by the prophetic. What commonly happens is that someone has seen an area in another person's life that needs to be changed and has tried to use prophecy to do that. Prophecy, however, is not always the proper vehicle for such work. Changing things in people's lives is both a pastoral and prophetic issue. While prophets draw us into the orbit of the grace and mercy of God, pastors enable us to respond to God at the everyday, ground level of our lives. We need a partnership between the two ministries. Good leadership promotes sound partnerships that support the work of the Holy Spirit.

Revelatory Protocol

In 1 Thessalonians 5:16–22, the apostle Paul laid out the New Testament protocol for dealing with revelatory prophecy: "*Rejoice always; pray without ceasing; in everything give thanks; for this is God's will for you in Christ Jesus. Do not quench the Spirit; do not despise prophetic utterances. But examine everything carefully; hold fast to that which is good; abstain from every form of evil.*"

Judging and weighing prophecy is extremely important because we need to separate the good from the bad. Paul's advice to "examine everything carefully" was merely reinforcing the procedures used by Old Testament prophets. Very few of the great prophetic words in Scripture were spontaneous words. Most were given after hours, days, and even weeks of prayer and meditation by the prophet. The only recording technology the ancient prophets had was the quill and scroll, so they painstakingly wrote down the prophecies they were given. In those days, one had to walk everywhere, so a prophet had plenty of time to think out exactly what he or she had to say.

When a prophet was preparing to give a correctional word to a king, he especially wanted to take care to ensure that the word had God's blessing. After all, a bad word to a king could result in imprisonment, torture, or even death. No one can blame the prophet for wanting to make sure he was going to die for a good reason! So the words were carefully recorded, considered, and rehearsed before they were delivered. Many prophets had secretaries and associates who acted as scribes for them; Jeremiah, for example, had Baruch to write out his words. One can almost imagine a little old prophet, walking to Jerusalem to give the word of his life, muttering it out loud over and over again, working to get it just right. He spoke the word out of a deep well of prayer, meditation, and often fasting.

When the days are evil, all Christians need to be quickened in the life of Christ

God builds in time for us to judge and weigh the prophetic. He will never give a prophetic word that has to be implemented immediately; such an act flows against His nature and the precedent He has set out in Scripture. The Holy Spirit loves the prophetic process too much to sidestep it. As a guiding principle, revelatory prophecy needs to be checked out privately before it is given publicly because there is a governmental principle at stake. While these words can bring tremendous release, they can also cause immense harm. Because a wrong revelatory word can cause difficulty and damage, we must work it through with our church's leaders beforehand. Revelatory prophecy, especially if it includes correction or direction, needs to have the prior approval of leaders of the church, because whatever we hear from the Lord needs to be confirmed through the whole body of Christ. Prophets cannot give revelatory words with the same freedom and innocence as they do inspirational words.

Tension and Paradox

Certain things happen when someone stands up and gives a major, directional word to a church that has not been cleared or approved beforehand with the leaders. It immediately causes consternation because two camps form around the word: one of people who like it, and one of people who don't. This is inevitable, as there are two types of people in church: present people and future people. Present people have ministries that are focused on the here and now; they live in the moment. Pastoral ministry, for example, is generally preoccupied with the now. They see present needs and respond to them. Future people are more visionary and focused on the long-term. In whatever they do today, they are looking ahead to tomorrow. They are prophetic in their outlook, focused on dreaming of what the church could become.

There is no movement without tension

When directional prophecy comes, it drops into the tension between the present and the future. Prophets create tension, but this tension doesn't necessarily mean something is wrong. It means that something is happening! It is impossible to move without tension. No one can grip anything without tensing their muscles. Nor is tension all-encompassing. When I relax in a chair and reach out to pick up my coffee cup, the part of me that is in motion is tense while the remainder of my body is at rest.

This is typical of the body of Christ anywhere in the world. All ministries bring tension into the mix of relationships, organizations, and human desire. We must be careful that when that tension occurs it does not become a friction. We take the issues that may potentially divide us and put them on one side. This is a time to renew our friendships, allowing the Holy Spirit to ease the friction. Yet we must remember that we cannot hold onto something in the Spirit without tension being present.

Tension indicates that something is happening in the church. The future and present camps are not the product of prophecy; they exist before a word is given. Both are absolutely vital to the health of a body, because church itself is a paradox — two seemingly conflicting ideas contained in the same truth.

We are told that church is both a building and a body. A building is rigid, inflexible, and unchanging. A body is the complete opposite! It is fluid, flexible, and constantly changing.

One relates to relationships, the other to our functionality. In our friendships our love for one another is non-negotiable. It is rigid, inflexible, and unchanging. Love is a constant.

The way we operate church however is within the framework of a vision that is fluid, full of flexibility, and always open to change as we walk with the Lord in occupied territory.

Sadly the church has mixed up these two requirements. Relationships are fluid, changing, and temporary. We have Kleenex relationships that are used once or twice then thrown away. We let go of each other too easily. We can see people as objects to possess, acquire, and control.

Our vision and method of operating as church becomes rigid and inflexible. We regard history and tradition as inviolate. We act to preserve something that we don't want to change even though we live in a world that is constantly changing.

God's nature is like a building. It is constant, consistent, and unchanging. His methodologies however are fluid, flexible, and require continuous adjustment so that His plans and purpose can be wholly fulfilled in the earth. Prophets understand paradox and are able to work within the extremes of truth to determine the presence and the purpose of God.

We must have people of the present and people of the future. If we didn't have now people, nothing would ever get done. But we also need those future people, the ones who will be first out there when God breathes on something new. Directional prophecy can polarize these camps by coming into the tension created by the paradox of now, but not yet. The King is coming, the King is here: this is the crux of that now, but not yet, paradox. A healthy relationship between the two groups is vital to the success of a church. While we begin to explore out there, we must maintain what we have in here.

Every church has periods of consolidation and periods of development. Future people must submit to the now work within current conditions. In turn, present people must enable future people to explore and be part of the realignment that sometimes must occur. No church is supposed to stay the same forever. We're all on a journey toward God, moving toward an ideal that God has set aside for us in the Spirit.

If we do not know how to give directional prophecies properly, we will create huge problems for ourselves. We will not understand the tension that comes. Often the enemy seeks to exploit these times of tension by trying to divide us. Fortunately, God has His own agenda rooted in love, honor, and faithfulness. The enemy cannot sustain an attack when we allow God to bring us even closer together in times of trouble. The enemy makes the issue seem more vital than it actually is, but the Holy Spirit seeks to elevate love and friendship to new heights. Unity in the Spirit is more precious to God than any issue.

The flow and the ebb of the Spirit are both vital

To get to that place of unity, we may have to put the issue to the side for a given period of time. We can always pick it up again, but our first priority must be love and friendship. We renew our relationships, strengthen our love for each other, and reaffirm our commitment to one another. We cannot use friendship and unity as an excuse not to move forward at all. This is dishonest and dishonorable to the Lord. The love of God and our unity is a vehicle to explore the future, not a barrier to prevent it occurring!

Issues must be faced in the right spirit and in a manner that releases the Holy Spirit and glorifies the Father. Only when this has been achieved to the satisfaction of the Holy Spirit can we reexamine the issue. Ninety percent of the time, we will discover that the issue has lost its power to divide us. The enemy cannot sustain an attack when the love of God is at the forefront of our hearts. We are all capable, in the inspiration of the Holy Spirit, of being gracious and humble, loving and kind. When these aspects of God's character prevail in our hearts, agreement is but a short step away. Friendship has grown between us, we have fellowshipped this thing through, and now we can look at the issue without division. Otherwise, prophetic ministry can be an open door for the demonic to enter our churches by using the division it causes.

To ease this tension and ensure that we are unified in what God is seeking to do, revelatory words that affect the judgment and direction of a church should follow this protocol:

1. Write out the prophecy as clearly as possible, focusing on its main point, and share it humbly with the leaders of the church.
2. Leave it with them, trusting them and the Lord to judge and weigh it. Stay available to the leaders for further discussion and consideration.
3. Accept the method of delivery they decide on.

Sharing It With Leaders

Even though I am recognized by my church as a prophet, I would never dream of standing up on a Sunday morning, going to the microphone, and delivering a spontaneous, directional word to the body. While my friends and colleagues in leadership would probably be okay with me doing so, I simply wouldn't. They trust me with their lives and I have earned the right over the years to say what I want from the platform, but even still, I would never exercise that freedom. I wouldn't do it because of my relationship with my friends, my relationship with God, and my relationship with the prophetic people I am teaching.

God has not given me the outright, overall leadership of our church. He's given that to my dear friend David Crone. We both understand that I am serving the Lord with my gift, my life, and my ministry. But I am also serving David with my gift and my ministry. It is very important to me that David succeeds in the things that God has given him to do. I want to be a part of that success. If it came down to a choice between him succeeding and me succeeding, I would want him to succeed. If there was only one blessing left for the two of us, I would want David to have it. This is what kingdom life is all about. We are in this thing together. His success is my success.

There should be no such thing as enemies in the church. If there are, it is the enemy at work using our carnality and we need to deal with it. It doesn't matter if it is people against people — the origin is devilish. The enemy is against us, and if he can turn one of us against another then he has formed a beach that he can exploit. In order for us to deal with some of those issues, we need to first deal with the enemy. After taking care of him, we can work things out between us. Enmity should not exist in church.

A great exercise to try is to look up all of the "one anothers" in the New Testament. There are many: "Love one another," "Honor one another," "Prefer one another," "Provoke one another to love and good works," "Pray for one another," "Encourage one another." The list goes on and on. We practice the presence of God in our relationships, not in our meetings. God comes to friendships mostly. If we practice the "one anothers" we will have friendships that can attract the presence of God into our very midst. They are a guarantee of habitation!

When we forfeit the "one anothers" lifestyle of the kingdom, we downgrade God's dream of living with His people (habitation) to settle for an experience that merely involves visitation. Revival is merely a visitation — a much lower form of spirituality than the Father intends. This is the very essence of church life and a reflection of the attitude of the Godhead.

Is your church a place of habitation or merely visitation for God?

The Father can say about the Son, "This is my beloved Son. Listen to Him." He promoted Jesus as the focal point of their work. What did Jesus do? He walked with men and turned the glory back to the Father: "I'm only doing what My Father in Heaven is doing," He said. "I'm only saying what My Father in Heaven is saying." Then Jesus made an astounding comment to His disciples: "It's better for you if I go away, because then the Holy Spirit can come."

The disciples must have been stunned. How could something be better than walking with Jesus Himself? What could He mean? Jesus simply knew that the next phase of their lives would be better led by the Holy Spirit. The Spirit is brilliant at teaching, guiding, empowering, releasing, and building us. When the Spirit comes, He specifically speaks of Jesus, revealing and magnifying Him.

The Godhead promotes, honors, and prefers one another. They all bless and speak highly of each other. They represent one another. This is kingdom life, and it is the attitude and perspective that we need in the church. When we carry that same Godlike attitude, we readily submit to leadership and share our revelatory prophecy with them first.

In Romans 13:1–5, Paul made it clear that we are subject to governing authorities, whether secular or sacred.

> *Every person is to be in subjection to the governing authorities. For there is no authority except from God, and those which exist are established by God. Therefore whoever resists authority has opposed the ordinance of God; and they who have opposed will receive condemnation upon themselves. For rulers are not a cause of fear for good behavior, but for evil. Do you want to have no fear of authority? Do what is good and you will have praise from the same; for it is a minister of God to you for good. But if you do what is evil, be afraid; for it does not bear the sword for nothing; for it is a minister of God, an avenger who brings wrath on the one who practices evil. Therefore it is necessary to be in subjection, not only because of wrath, but also for conscience' sake.*

We need to have respect for leadership so that we earn the right to speak. When we partner with leaders and intercede for them, we can ask the Lord to infuse our relationship with the spirit of partnership. If we give ourselves in partnership, partnership is given to us. But we must act first! Peter echoed Paul's words in 1 Peter 2:13–17:

> *Submit yourselves for the Lord's sake to every human institution, whether to a king as the one in authority, or to governors as sent by him for the punishment of evildoers and the praise of those who do right. For such is the will of God that by doing right you may silence the ignorance of foolish men. Act as free men, and do not use your freedom as a covering for evil, but use it as bond-slaves of God. Honor all people, love the brotherhood, fear God, honor the king.*

When God gives us a word for our church, we must make sure we present it the right way, with accuracy, humility, and kindness. Part of my role in Vacaville, California is being a member of a leadership think tank. Together, we dialogue and ask God about the future. We look three years down the road to see what is coming next. What is it that we are becoming? What is going to happen in the city over the next three years that we need to prepare for? Several times a year, we meet in order to anticipate the future.

If I get a directional word from the Lord, I almost always write it out. Usually, I use bullet points so that it is easy to read. Then I make an appointment with David and the rest of the team to give them the word. When sharing a revelatory word with leadership, it is very helpful to write down as much as possible. At the very least, we must try to encapsulate the main headlines of the prophecy. This facilitates the communication process and makes it easier for the leadership to understand and receive the prophetic word.

When I give the word to them, I do it as humbly as possible: "This is what I feel like the Lord is saying to me in regard to the direction of the church. I feel like this might carry some implications for what we do." They listen, and we pray together. Quite often, they have laid hands on me and blessed me. I try to answer any of the questions they have, especially when they are trying to clarify something. It is a good idea where possible to record these conversations and get the tapes transcribed, and then go back and read over them so the word can be properly judged and weighed.

> ***All partnerships are based on mutual love, service, and humility***

At that point, the accountability for the prophetic word passes from me to them. They are now accountable for it.

Leadership Involvement

When we turn the word over to our leaders, accountability shifts to them. They must give account to the Lord for their response to the prophetic. At the very least, they must take the prophecy seriously enough to judge it. What they do with the word is now their own spiritual responsibility. If it is a true word from the Lord and they ignore it, they will have to bear that before the Lord some day. What they do with it is between them and the Father.

We must leave the prophecy with them — we are no longer accountable for it. We are only accountable for the way we presented it. We may want to check on its progress as the leaders submit the word to the judging process. That is quite natural and normal, because sometimes our sense of burden does not leave with the delivery of the word. However, we must take care that we display no sense of arrogance or of checking up on people. Leadership, in turn, needs to be gracious and patient in the process. Both parties need a large measure of humility and understanding; we must be in fellowship together in the situation.

Failure to follow this principle can cause a lot of strife. I have worked with numerous churches to heal the damage done by poor prophetic ministry and poor leadership response to excellent prophecy. Seeing these situations first-hand was one of the reasons I wrote *Developing Your Prophetic Gifting*, set up my schools of prophecy, and wrote this series of books. Too much damage is being done in the local church in the name of prophetic ministry. A controlling leadership that does not allow revelatory prophecy or misuses it can be just as deadly. A very unhealthy tension can exist between prophetic ministry and local leadership that can be exploited by unscrupulous people and by the enemy. It doesn't have to be this way. Over the years, I have built a relationship of trust with David and the other leaders in Vacaville. It is easy to leave a word with them because I trust them so much.

The bigger the word, the more judging and weighing should go on. I have given churches certain words of such large magnitude that the leaders have looked for outside confirmation. To get that, they have alerted prophetic ministries they know and trust, told them that a word of direction has been given to our church, and asked them to pray about it. We don't share the details of the original word with these outsiders, but instead ask them to pursue God and tell us whatever they hear.

Confirmation is a major part of New Testament prophecy

I have been on both sides of that confirmation process. Many years ago, friends in another church had received a number of prophetic words from inside their own congregation. These words were directional and would create an agenda within the work for some time to come. The leaders had received so many words that they were finding it hard to be objective and to judge them properly. They contacted me and asked me to wait on the Lord with a view to providing some external input into their situation.

They didn't tell me anything about the content of the previous prophecies. They were seeking to use my input as confirmation by laying my external perspective alongside their internal prophecies. They asked me to come and give my prophetic input at a specially arranged meeting.

I started to pray but found that what I was getting for the church was so specific and directional that I called my friend and told him I couldn't do the meeting. I knew I had the platform to prophesy, but the word I had was so focused that I needed him to hear it first so he could judge and weigh it. He told me they were quite happy for me to do the evening as planned. I appreciated that but I was still unhappy. It took a lot, but I finally convinced him to let me meet with him and his elders to discuss it and go from there.

When I met with the leaders and shared the prophetic words I had received, a terrific excitement took hold of them. Apparently, not only had the Holy Spirit confirmed many of the previous words, He had also taken them several stages further and actually given them a full strategy for the next five years.

After some time in prayer, we realized that we needed to plan an evening for the whole church and create an environment where everyone could become impregnated with the prophetic word of the Lord. That meeting has become a landmark in the life of that church. They have grown significantly in Spirit and numbers and are now increasing their influence throughout their region.

A prophetic word can be so big for a church leadership team that it feels like they are stepping off a cliff. But we still have to leave it with them. If I still have a burden for the word, I may ask if they need anything, but even in that they still carry responsibility for the word.

Not every word I give is delivered to the wider body. Many have never been spoken out but have still become part of the fabric of the church. Sometimes a word confirms the new sense of direction a leadership team feels and gives them confidence in what they are about to attempt. Some words are better put into teaching or preaching and are presented with scriptural principles by our speakers. It does not matter how these words are used as long as we are all conspiring together to do the right thing before the Lord.

Some words should be given to leaders and intercessors to be prayed through before the throne of God. Not every prophecy is for full public consumption. When we submit everything to the Holy Spirit, He gives us wisdom to know how to handle each individual situation.

In many churches, some words, even good ones, can be simply rejected or ignored. If the leadership is not ready or willing, the tension from the prophecy will cause difficulties. Unfortunately, it is all too easy to dismiss the prophecy and cast the prophet in the role of troublemaker. It is an easy way out of a potential dilemma and has been used on many occasions. This flows from a lack of understanding about how prophecy actually works and causes many conflicts and misunderstandings. The prophet is blamed for causing trouble because it is easier than facing the issue of change that prophecy often releases into the church.

All prophecy stimulates adjustment

Frustration exists between the "ideal" of where God is taking a church, which the prophet sees, and the "actual" of where the church is now, which the leadership sees. Prophecy paints a new picture, broadens our horizons, and lifts our vision, but leaders deal mostly with where the church is now.

Leadership Involvement

Both parties must occupy that middle ground of frustration righteously. If, as the prophetic person involved, we move out of a sense of frustration with events or rejection in the ministry, then it becomes easier to prophesy our own opinions. We must ensure that we are not living with any negative influences over our own lives that can taint the prophetic word. It is perfectly possible to have a positive word about the future of the church, prophetically see a new horizon, and proclaim the new things that God is going to bring into the work.

Real prophecy will always provoke a change

However, our frustration and negativity can get the better of us. Instead of prophesying blessing and showing the new things of God to lift our collective vision, we can give into our negativity. We speak to the actual while pointing at the ideal: "I have this against you, says the Lord, because you are not this!"

Leaders can also be at fault in this area. There is a need to care for and love our prophetic people. They need accurate, kind feedback within a framework of relationship and discipleship. Above all, we need to establish a leadership that has at least a basic understanding of how prophecy works. I am amazed by how many times the leaders of a church hosting a prophetic conference have not attended the event themselves. That is startlingly bad form and a missed opportunity for leaders to grow in their understanding of the prophetic. It is essential that we know how to handle that middle ground of frustration. These guidelines apply to everyone, regardless of our "status" within the prophetic ministry. We must be committed to waiting for confirmation on prophetic words we receive.

If a word is confirmed by the leadership, the next step is to set out a strategy on how to cooperate with the Lord to bring the word to fruition. It is vital that leaders and prophets ask themselves within any work, "How do we introduce significant prophetic words into the church?" Unfortunately, Scripture has no clear guidelines to offer on this matter. We are left with two extremes: the purely spontaneous, off-the-cuff word, and the prepared, rehearsed prophetic input. Both are equally valid; most times it is a question of both together rather than choosing one method over the other. It is good to have a prepared framework through which the Holy Spirit can breathe and add to that word in a spontaneous manner.

Delivery of a Word

Directional words, having been judged and weighed beforehand, can benefit from a large investment of prayer, guidance, and preparation from the Holy Spirit. The people feel safe knowing that directional prophecy has already been subjected to evaluation. When that word is released, it will create an immediate faith impact in the hearts of the congregation.

If we work the other way and bring a directional word into the work without weighing it first, we will not get the response we expect. First, this method opens the church to the danger of a non-accountable prophetic gifting sowing disorder. Second, the response will be muted, because the word still needs to be judged and weighed. A gap will open between the word being given and the word being approved. Even then, we will have to plan the successful entrance of the word into the hearts of the people. It is a little like giving a plateful of mouth-watering food to a hungry man and then whisking it away to ensure it has been cooked properly. By the time he gets the food back, it may well be cold!

All prophecy must lead to process

If we can judge the word prior to public delivery, we can safeguard the flock and create an environment that is dynamic in bringing the prophetic word into the work. Boundaries that are set by the Holy Spirit do not quench His ministry but instead help us fulfill His purpose. Prophecy requires a response. The method of delivery must correspond in some way to the desired outcome. A smart leadership team will set out a strategy to release and build on the word.

Directive words always have an impact on the body. It might be a significant shift in direction, or just a small course correction, but it will still touch certain groups within a church. Not every Christian likes change, and we have to be sensitive to that. Most people, however, can handle a series of small adjustments during a lengthy journey.

We need a strategy to bring the word in. In practice, when the senior leadership wants to release a prophetic word to the wider body, it is good to call an extraordinary meeting of all of the leaders in the church. Gather the core leaders and ministries and spend an evening unpacking the word. Worship together and then give the word, pointing out that the leaders and elders of the church have been weighing it for the past time period. "This is what we've done with this word: we have judged it, we have weighed it, we have tested it, and we feel it is right. But we want to be sure, and we want to share it with you first so we can pray about it together."

Questions are asked and answered, implications are considered. Over the next few weeks, the broader leadership circle prays and meditates. After that, a full church meeting can be called, with everyone who is part of the home body invited. Again, we can explain the process and present the word: "We have been praying over this word for the past three months, weighed it, and tested it. We have brought all the leaders of the church together, asked questions, and have come to the feeling that this is a word from the Lord for us. We believe, without a doubt, that God is calling us to this."

At that point, we can share the word and talk about its implications on all of us. We make sure everyone receives a tape of that evening meeting plus a written transcript of the word. We are intentional about following the word through.

Over the next few weeks, our cell groups work through the word, pray about it, and think about it. Everybody knows that this prophecy is where we are going and what we are doing. Collectively, the church judges and weighs the word.

When we deal with a major directive word, we need to minimize the relational tensions that can occur in revelatory prophecy. We work together as partners in the church and kingdom, submitting to one another for the sake of Christ. This process may seem lengthy and overcooked, however, a number of things are taking place that are the lifeblood of any progressive church.

When people are empowered to dream they will own their future

First, we are having a dialogue about the future which means we can upgrade our present–future relationship with the Holy Spirit. Second, we are developing our partnership and prayer to a new level of cooperation. Third, the maturing process is being advanced in a way that preaching and teaching cannot generate. Fourth, everyone's voice is being heard. We are enfranchising the people to anticipate the future. We govern by consultation, not consensus. When people are empowered to talk about the future they own it because they have contributed to it. It is always the process that makes us rich, never just the outcome. A church that processes together will always proceed together!

Delivery of the word is a key ingredient to seeing it fulfilled. Only mature and tested people should give revelatory, directive words in public. There are times when somebody has a revelatory word which is accurate but because of circumstances in their own life, it would be inappropriate for them to be the one that gives the word in public. To be in visible prophetic ministry, we the messengers have to be as good as the message itself. What we don't want is two-thirds of a church rejecting a prophetic word because they know the prophet is not living their entire life to please God. We don't reject the word, but we do let them know that they will not be asked to give it publicly.

The Pharisees were the dream thieves of their day

We still give credit to the individual who originally gave the word, but we protect it, and them, by having someone else deliver it. This always happens after a conversation with the prophetic voice. When it comes to giving the word, we will often say, "Would you mind if so-and-so gave it in your place? We just don't want to put you under too much pressure right now by having you up there publicly in a situation that might cause you some embarrassment. We want to safeguard the word, but we also want to safeguard your reputation." We want to produce prophetic people whose lifestyles are capable of being honorable and above reproach.

Delivering Difficult Words

Some prophetic words are tougher than others to give, but we still have to deliver them. I have worked hard at learning how to give such words while making people laugh. I draw people into wanting such a love for God that they accept the challenge if it is going to help them get there.

It is possible to give hard words without offending everyone. Unfortunately, it is not something that can be taught through a six point strategy. It takes practice, humility, and sensitivity to who God is for us. Our journey crafts us into the type of prophet we are. It comes out of what God is doing in us and whatever burden He has placed on our hearts.

The word has to be given gently, no matter how harsh it is. It has to be willing to yield — we have to be open to being challenged on it. This is where leaving it with the church leadership is so valuable. None of us ever receive a full word: "*For we know in part and we prophesy in part,*" as Paul said in 1 Corinthians 13:9. What often happens in the judging and weighing process is that God reveals more revelation to the leaders involved, allowing them to add to it, and giving them a stake in it. Suddenly, they come alive.

A few years ago, I gave a word to a church leadership body that included one individual known for his caution. I had nicknamed him "Mr. Cautious" because he was always the one suggesting patience, waiting, and thinking. I loved that about him: he was just being true to himself, and the community valued that. I gave the word and honestly expected him to suggest that everyone wait on it. After a lengthy discussion, we decided as a group to meet again the next day to further consider the prophecy.

Mr. Cautious arrived the next morning and stunned me. "Well," he said, "I had a dream last night." The dream and his interpretation fit perfectly with the prophetic word. I love that! This was the first time something like that had happened to him and he was absolutely thrilled. It changed the way he judged and weighed words.

God is always doing a hundred more things than we think He is doing in a particular situation. Our role is to be willing to yield to Him. We don't need to defend our own prophecy — that's not our job. We are not called to explain the gospel, but instead to proclaim it. We are not trying to make people understand who God is, but are instead called to say, "This is who He is."

> *It is such a delightful privilege to trust the Father*

People can take it or leave it, for our only job is to proclaim it and trust that the Holy Spirit will come and make the proclamation real. The moment we try and explain God, everyone loses interest. It is boring to rationalize the Almighty. We can't explain the inexplicable, so why try? Instead, we proclaim Jesus, what He is like, and what He is doing.

Proclamation is like a key in the door of the hearts of the people who hear it. It opens them to thinking in a way that explanation never can. Kindness needs to be at the core of all of our verbal interaction. We are supposed to be good to one another and to ourselves. The grace of God allows us to feel good about who we are. We can like who we are in God.

Becoming Christlike is a process full of mercy and good fruit. Everything we do to each other has to be godly. Our conversations must somehow draw people closer to who Jesus really is. The way we speak with people, the way we connect, the way we handle ourselves: this all communicates who we are in Christ. We need to remove all double standards and hypocrisy from our life and be teachable in all things.

One of my mentors used to say to me, "Graham, the humble man has an advantage over all other men. No one can put you down." If we humble ourselves, God can exalt us. But if we glorify ourselves, God will have to humble us so that we are not lost to the calling.

The fruit of righteousness is sown in peace by those who make peace. Second Peter 1:4 calls us "partakers of the divine nature." If we partake in it, we must transmit it by giving it away to those around us.

The church has got to become prophetic, full of words that cut across where we are and what is happening. I remember going to a church in northern England for the first time. My first evening there, I met with the elders. I was very casual, even leaning on a stack of boxes in the pastor's office. "Do you sense anything prophetic over this church?" the pastor asked me. "Oh yes," I answered. "This is what I hear the Lord saying. This church is like a wheel, like a hub. God is going to give you eight church plants around this area. Your influence is going to go through all of these spokes throughout the region. This church will give birth to eight churches." I then went on to describe each church, its influence, and measure of rule in the region.

It is the purpose of prophecy to challenge the status quo and provoke growth

Great word, but not at all what the pastor wanted to hear. He didn't want a mother church with eight daughter churches; he wanted a mega church of ten thousand people in his current location. I later found out that he had just published a vision statement that included his plan to build a mega church. In fact, the very boxes I was leaning on contained the leaflets explaining that mega church vision! He was not happy with me. He quickly left the church office and I didn't see him again that weekend.

Still, he went ahead with his vision and the church split over it. Naturally, I was blamed for the conflict because of my prophetic word, despite the fact that the split was actually caused by the pastor's refusal to share his vision with his leaders before taking it to the printer. The pastor took the people who wanted a mega church and left to build it, but it never came about. I stayed and worked for four years with the people who remained and now, thirteen years later, that church numbers eight hundred, with eight daughter churches ranging in size from fifty to one-hundred and twenty. All of them are still growing.

Delivering a public prophetic word is a difficult task for an introvert like me. But even those of us who are shy by nature can have a larger than life personality because we represent someone who is so compellingly awesome. Prophetic ministry always leads the Lord to be magnified in the hearts and minds of people. The only way we can accurately describe Jesus is to use superlatives. The only way we can mention Him in conversation is with a delightful smile on our face. Church would be so much grander if we would learn to live together under the smile of God. The gospel is the best news of all, and we must be astounded by the wonder of it.

How Ministries Interact

God is keenly interested in seeing ministries connect, network, and partner with one another. He has not called any of us to be a ministry apart from everyone else. He has set us in the body of Christ and expects us to team with certain people. This is especially important for prophetic ministries. By working together, we can flesh out the prophecy we receive, building on what one another is hearing and doing.

On some days, I have received so much detail and content about a specific thing that I don't know what to do with it all. The receiving of revelation and the power to deal with it are often two separate exercises. There are times when a prophet will take the revelation, try to interpret it himself, and speak it publicly, but nothing happens. It just doesn't work. I know firsthand how frustrating that can be; one even wonders if he's hearing God at all.

There are no lone voices, just poor team players

But maybe the issue isn't about us mishearing God. Maybe it is about God wanting us to partner with someone else to fully develop and deliver the word. Who is God joining you to in your local church? Who has He welded you together with? Are there ministries around you with which you need to partner and bless?

When something isn't working properly, I have learned to step back and ask the Lord if there is anything I'm not fully seeing. Quite often I discover that it is a partnership issue, and I need to find the person I am supposed to be working with in that regard.

A friend of mine once explained this dynamic very clearly to me. "Graham," he said, "you've got a very highly developed radar, but you don't send the radar up to shoot enemy planes down. You have to find someone who has got the weapon, the power, and the anointing to actually deal with what you are seeing." This metaphor released me to be myself in prophecy, and not try to be all things to all people. It also reinforced my belief that the Lord wants us to all be good team players and to get to know the people God has partnered us with.

Interpretation

Interpretation is a key part of every prophetic word. It is very possible to hear the Lord perfectly but misinterpret what He has said and, therefore, botch the word. Faulty interpretation can completely derail us.

I once took a call from a man named John from a church where I had a lot of relationship. John had a situation in his life that the elders couldn't resolve, so they told him to call me for my perspective. Apparently, a prophetic minister based overseas had told John that he had seen a picture of him dressed in army fatigues, walking up and down a beach with a metal detector. The prophet interpreted this as meaning that John was being given a ministry in spiritual warfare and would be used to detect buried enemy activity. He would be deliberately looking for the devices of the enemy in people's lives. He was also going to be used to defuse those devices. Essentially, he would be surrounded by demonic activity in the world and would become a target. He would have to learn how to fight off direct demonic intervention into his life and family. Not the most cheerful word I've ever heard!

Even a broken clock is right twice a day!

The problem arose because the interpretation brought a tremendous amount of confusion, fear, and uncertainty. There was no progression in that word from any previous prophetic word John had ever received. It was completely disconnected from anything he had done in ministry up until that point. It wasn't necessarily wrong, but a deep divide did exist between the actual situation and this prophetic ideal. John felt no peace about it, and his close friends could not witness to it. His wife was also extremely worried.

Things began to turn sour at home. His children began waking in the night screaming; horrendous smells would come out of nowhere. The kids complained of seeing monsters in the hallway and on the stairs. They said they sometimes felt a "presence" that terrified them.

The family was at a loss. The one thing they didn't do was question the interpretation of the picture. They thought that this might be the price John would have to pay to enter this level of ministry. It tore him apart; he cried when we spoke on the phone. I asked him for the picture revelation only, not the interpretation, and told him I would pray.

The Lord showed me this interpretation: "The beach is the church, and the Lord is going to use John like a mettle detector." Mettle is an old English word derived from the time of knights, armor, and sword fights. It means "quality of spirit, courage, temperament, to encourage a person to greater effort, to release zeal and determination." Thus the old saying, "being on your mettle," is an exhortation to be the best you can be.

Instead of having John looking for enemy activity and defusing enemy devices, the Lord was sending him on a treasure hunt. He would sweep through the church, looking for treasure in people's lives — the rich deposit of Christ's love and care and the heavenly deposit of gift, power, and anointing that resides in Christians' hearts. Some of this treasure may be buried under layers of sin, low self-esteem, unbelief, and ignorance. However, John would bring it to the surface and clean it off. By polishing it, he would reveal the beauty of Christ. The Lord was giving him a ministry on the fringe of the church where there are many people who feel they have missed God, have lost any significance, and are going nowhere. The Lord would send John to detect what the Spirit was doing in the lives of those fringe people and bring it to the surface.

Interpretations are like planes: it's important to get on the right one!

When I gave this perspective to John and the elders, the overwhelming feeling was that this was the correct interpretation. We then moved forward in prayer against the activity of the enemy, confident that those things were not part of the price for his ministry, but that the enemy had simply taken advantage of his situation.

Words are powerful and can create things. They can bring a blessing or a curse, understanding or confusion, faith or despair. As we took authority and spoke the right interpretation into John's life, we saw God move in His situation and return things to normal. The revelation was absolutely right, but the interpretation was completely off track. Do not be tempted to strive to manufacture an interpretation when one is not clear. Very often we find that people have the uncanny ability to mold the interpretation they prefer around a particular prophetic word.

One of the funny things about the prophetic is that God will sometimes show us things that don't make a lick of sense. I was in South Africa for a conference once when the Lord highlighted a woman in the crowd and gave me one line of prophecy for her. I honestly thought it was one of those situations where I would give my one line and the Lord would then give me reams more. I had her stand up, opened my mouth, and gave my sentence: "The Lord says, 'What happened to your mother won't happen to you."

And that was it. There was no more revelation coming. I looked at her and said, "I'm awfully sorry but that's all I've got." The woman burst into tears.

"My mother died when she was thirty-seven-and-a-half, and my older sister died when she was thirty-seven-and-a-half," she told me later. "I'm thirty-seven next week and I'm scared."

A word is sometimes made supernatural because of the situation we speak into. The word can be completely ordinary but may pack a punch we had never dreamed of. That night we realized that God wanted to break something generational off this woman. We prayed for her, and now she is in her late forties.

If we do not have the interpretation to a particular word, we need to pray with the individual that one will come. Sometimes I give words and have no understanding why I'm saying them. I am just being obedient to God. I have not received the interpretation, but I know I have permission at this point in time to give this prophetic word, so I obey. The person who is receiving the word doesn't always understand it. Other people around them may say, "We know what this means," but, sometimes, no one knows what it means! What we have to do then is take that particular prophetic input and put it on a shelf.

The Shelf

My American friend John Paul Jackson and I were once doing a conference together in England, and I asked him to pray for some friends of mine. I love working with John Paul, because we have the same passion for Jesus and the prophetic. I was grateful when he agreed to pray for some of the people who were helping me in my ministry, and I was excited to see them have the opportunity to be blessed.

My friend David was one of the people John Paul prayed for. "In three months, you will be standing before princes and kings, and living in a different country," John Paul told David.

David and I were shocked, our jaws on the floor. The word had come out of the clear blue sky. He hadn't been thinking about overseas work. In fact, he was very happy in his domestic job.

But this word wasn't on the shelf very long. The very next week, David was headhunted by a major agency and ended up working in the United Arab Emirates for several Arab princes and sheiks. Just three months passed from the moment of prophecy to it being fulfilled.

Prophecy opens up the possibility of increased participation and cooperation with the Holy Spirit. We receive an agenda that must be carefully worked through with the Father. There are questions that naturally occur after prophecy is delivered. Prophecy provokes questions. Questions form our agenda for change.

I prophesied over a young, developing evangelist regarding his future ministry. The word involved signs and wonders, miracles, and great provision of faith. We must at the very least ask, "What kind of person must I become now in order for this identity and destiny to unfold?"

When the angel of the Lord visited the Danite woman and informed her she would have a son (Samson, Judges 13) she told her husband Manoah. He asked the Lord for confirmation and when it came he also asked this very important question: "*When your words come to pass, what shall be the boy's mode of life and his vocation?*" (13:12). What kind of person does my son need to become in order to fulfill his calling? This is the key to processing prophecy. Regarding the young evangelist, I knew that at the time of prophesying there was only a 30 percent chance of the prophecy coming to pass. He struggled financially. He was not a good giver and had problems living by faith and believing for financial provision.

Faith for finances is the shallow end of the miraculous. It's the place where we step into the extravagant nature of the Father. If he cannot get past this place, the young evangelist will never make it. He will be broken by the demands of the ministry as so many people before him. This is warfare and it's real.

Fortunately for him, he opened himself up to counsel. He put the word and his ministry on the shelf and worked hard on his relationship with the Holy Spirit. Using the prophecy as a guide we mapped out a development program for those characteristics and qualities required to move in a high level of supernatural anointing. He has never looked back but has gone from strength to strength in his spiritual lifestyle and his ministry.

We should encourage people to have a shelf where they put words that they do not understand or that have no fulfillment for where they are in life at that moment. God has spoken something, the fullness of which will be revealed in time. We are expecting an interpretation and a greater clarity as we prayerfully wait. Many times, I have had words that were delivered ahead of time so that people may, through a prayerful response, be made ready for what God is doing. Suddenly we are pitched into a set of circumstances that are now illuminated by the light of the prophetic word given some time previously.

I once gave a man a word that his job situation was going to change for the worse, and that his boss would turn against him and make his life so difficult that he would want to quit. The Lord, however, was going to teach him about trust, perseverance, rest, and fighting the enemy. He was to stand still under God's hand through this time of testing, and he would inherit a place of authority.

At that time, the man's cousin was his boss, and they were the best of friends. His initial reaction was that I had completely missed the word. I encouraged him to shelve it rather than dismiss it. Ironically, the word drove the two cousins to pray for the company, and for a while everything was better than ever. Several months later, though, his cousin moved to another job. The man who took over was violently opposed to Christianity. Eighteen months of hell followed his hiring as the new manager took every opportunity to get the Christian fired. During this time, the only thing the believer had to hold on to was the Lord's promise for the situation. Two years after the prophecy was given, the new manager was let go, and the Christian man elevated to his position.

In the early stages of the prophetic word, when it seemed that the exact opposite was occurring, the man needed to shelve the word rather than dismiss it completely. On that occasion, it was a great comfort to know that the Lord saw everything ahead of time. The prophetic word became a doorway from heaven to earth through which the Lord walked at the appropriate time. Being able to stand in our circumstances and declare, like Peter on the day of Pentecost, "This is that which was spoken," is a powerful weapon in our hand. The Lord is amazing in situations like that for His kindness is incredible.

I understand when people come forward looking for an interpretation after being given a revelatory prophecy. However, there are times when I don't have a clue what I meant. Never manufacture an interpretation, even if people try to push you into a corner for one. Be honest: "I don't actually know what I meant by that, but that's what I felt God was showing me. Let's pray together and as we seek the Lord, maybe an interpretation will come clear." I once had a word for a man that didn't become clear until two nights later when God gave him the interpretation in a dream. Interpretation is up to the Lord. He is big enough to take care of business like that.

Application: The Third Piece

A revelation, an interpretation, and the application can be given by three different people. That is why it is important that we don't look to prophecy alone for guidance, and why we should encourage people to have a shelf, write things down, and share them with other people. When it comes down to application, we need to be as clear as we possibly can within what God has given us. Some days, it won't be possible to give that application. In times like that, we need to be willing to humble ourselves and tell the individual we are praying for, "You know what, I haven't got a clue what I mean. This revelation is all I've got; I don't have anything else, but I am really happy to pray with you." I have found that most people appreciate this kind of honesty and usually take the word very seriously, despite the lack of obvious application.

Revelation can open up entire areas of people's lives. When I am prophesying, I don't always know what is happening in the individual's life, but the revelation can open something up that the Lord may want to touch and deal with.

A word of prophecy usually contains three parts: a word of knowledge that can open up the situation, a word of prophecy that can speak to it, and a word of wisdom that brings clarity as to how to proceed. In the application stage, I am often asking God for a word of wisdom: "Now Lord, what do we do? We've had a true revelation and an accurate interpretation, but where do we go from here?" Along with the application, I ask God who else should hear this word. I always try to encourage people to go and share the word I gave them with their pastor, small group leader, or another spiritually mature person. Prophecy given in a vacuum is not an option; that is one of the reasons I like prophetic words to be recorded, either on tape or paper.

In many prophecies, there are specific action points that need to be pursued. Every time a person gets a word of prophecy about his or her ministry, we need to discuss their character. Character may not have even been mentioned in the word, but that is irrelevant. All successful ministry has to be built on rock-solid character.

Timing is another question to ask the Lord about. We have to make sure people don't rush off, quit their jobs, and move into ministries before confirmation has occurred. I have seen that happen too many times before! People suddenly leave everything they have ever known and jump unprepared into ministry because they want it now. However, generally speaking, after the calling comes the training. When there is a prophetic call on someone's life, he or she has to go through a period of training and development.

I prophesied to a man that he would become a warrior who would fight great battles and be an overcomer. He would have a reputation for standing firm. He would be a man of courage and fortitude who would encourage others in the heat of battle.

His church leaders wanted to disavow the prophecy and have me disciplined. Apparently this individual had a present identity of being weak, spineless, and a worrier — not a warrior!

How can we love a God who transforms people, yet imagine that there are some people who cannot change? I met with this man and his leaders. I had one question to ask the guy. "If you had a choice between being the guy your leaders see and the man God sees, what would you choose?"

Always choose your best life! I gave him some advice on developing the character and persona of a warrior. I asked the leadership to provide some discipling to assist him with applying truth for the purpose of transformation. Interesting that not only did no one in the group volunteer to disciple the man, they didn't name any one else either.

Prophecy provides us with a divine acceleration. A quickening spirit that enables us to make years of growth in months time. Fortunately, this man became proactive in his own development. Several years later I met him and was astonished at what the Father had done. He was a different man, a different husband, and had a new anointing to overcome.

All prophecy has a moral imperative. If God is ordaining someone to be the next Billy Graham, that person better have a character at least as strong as his! When God gives a major word about calling, the very next thing that happens is a deep examination of our character. God wants to ensure that our character can come up to the same level as the anointing He wants to bestow on us.

We see this pattern again and again in Scripture. Joshua was obviously called to lead the Israelites, but he spent more than forty years working as Moses' assistant. Elisha spent years with Elijah. Jesus didn't enter ministry until He was thirty years old. The apostles followed him for three years before striking out on their own. Paul was mentored by Barnabas and, in turn, discipled men like Silas, Titus, and Timothy.

A high calling demands a level of character which often requires changes in our lives, relationships, perspectives, vision, and way we perceive God. To get us to that point, God often uses our circumstances to equip and prepare us.

The high calling actually works for and against us, because the very thing we're called to fight for is the thing God wants us to overcome in our own lives first.

At some point, every person who has ever received a prophetic word has felt like their lives have swung to the complete opposite of what the word promised. God posts His word for us and then works to get our character to the level necessary to see it fulfilled. In our humanity, it feels as though we fall further away from the word, but in actuality, we are drawing closer. Just as the darkest hour of night is right before dawn, so prophecy is often fulfilled directly after a hard time. A friend of mine puts it like this: "While we're standing there lost in praise and wonder over our future, our inheritance, and what God is doing with us, He trips us up, throws us into a dark room, and beats the living daylights out of us!"

Joseph received a prophetic vision that his father and brothers would bow before him. His life initially went in the opposite direction and he found himself in the bottom of a pit looking up at them!

To occupy the high office that the Lord had planned for him, Joseph must lose his pride, his arrogance and must learn dependency on God. All of the circumstances that occur after prophecy are usually to develop the person we need to become in order for God's plan to fully mature.

David received a word about becoming king "in time" over Israel. The prophecy mentioned nothing about him being chased around the desert by a megalomaniac; hiding out in caves with malcontents; and being married to a woman who would grow to despise him! Everything that David experienced before prophecy was fulfilled was training for reigning. Life takes us in the opposite direction initially, but the Lord is in charge of the overall picture.

The application stage is also an opportunity to search the prophecy for any conditions attached to it. We need to get people thinking. The best two questions we can ask of God are: "What does this mean for my life, circumstances, and development?" and "What must I do to cooperate with the Holy Spirit in this situation?" How do we align ourselves with God's will in the process so that we can receive the fulfillment of His will in the outcome?

Timing belongs to God, but preparation belongs to us. We have to cooperate with God in the preparation or we may never see that time actually come into being. I have had prophetic words for people like this one: "You should have been in this ministry three years ago, but you're not because you never took care of the preparation." That kind of word is a wake-up call to repent and seek the Lord.

If we do not take care of the preparation, all that happens is that the timing keeps getting put off. God feels, "I can't bring this person in now; I can't trust them with this yet." There is a difference between trusting God and being trusted by Him. We must pay attention and prepare every area of our lives for the fulfillment of the word, otherwise it may never come to pass. Many

Christians live with unfulfilled prophecy because they have never taken care of the preparation or response factors that God is looking for.

Prophecy is about possibility, not inevitability. If the word in your life is going to be fulfilled in its entirety, then you need to seriously consider what level of character, righteousness, and integrity God is going to demand of you in order for Him to fulfill it. It is a powerful thing to live in your prophetic word as it begins to come to pass; we step out of the preparation into the actuality of something unfolding. (There is a CD series called "Living Your Destiny" that deals with this very issue in great detail. Go to: www.brilliantbookhouse.com).

Our goal as prophetic people should not be to simply talk about what God wants to do; our goal is to bring people to the place where the word is fulfilled. Instead of saying "The King is coming," we should dream of prophesying that "The King is here."

Character: The All-Important Ingredient

None of us should want to be known only for our anointing. It is our character that truly matters in the eyes of God. We should never be impressed by anointing or anything except what we see of Jesus in a person's life. The most important thing is the revelation of Jesus Christ they present. If that Christ-likeness isn't present, it doesn't matter how anointed they are or how powerful their ministry is — their ministry will end in ruin.

Anointing has led as many people astray as any enemy activity. The anointing to preach, teach, lead, or minister is only half of the equation. Anointing without a Christlike nature will damage people and ourselves. We can tear down with our character what God has built through our gift. If our Christian leaders are not established in who God is and what He is like, we might want to reconsider if we should be walking with that person. At the very least, we should ask the Lord a few questions: "Is this safe for me? Will You protect me? Do You want me to stay here?" All of us only have one life, and we have to make it count. This isn't a dress rehearsal; it's the big show. If God wants you in a specific place, it does not matter what their character is for you are there to make a difference in one way or another. You may have a particular job in that situation, a role to fulfill, something to contribute. Just do it in a godly, integral fashion.

We must all serve a Laban before we can appreciate an Abraham. There are many Laban-like leaders in the body of Christ. There are people who manipulate and use others for their own benefit. They take advantage of our ethics, our favor, and our desire to fully serve the Lord. They have their own agenda and see people around them as gifts of God to enable them to succeed. Real leaders see themselves as gifts of God to enable their people to succeed and fulfill their dreams. Never be impressed by anointing, but be impressed by what you see of Christ in people.

People talk about character being more important than gift. Actually it's a paradox. Both are equally as important as the other. The issue is one of precedent. In any given situation, whichever one is most required sets the precedent for what the Father wants to be and do in the circumstances.

Character and gifting is about being in the Lord and doing what He is doing. When we abandon either one of these elements we create a deficient view of God's personality and charisma.

Our morality does not stand still, but either gets better or worse. Scripture is littered with the stories of people who had great anointing but squandered their characters. Balaam clearly heard from God, but obviously had a less than perfect character. He was a prophet but he led people into great sin. King Saul was a man who prophesied with such depth that his countrymen made a proverb about it, but he ended his life in a web of murder, deceit, and witchcraft. The church at Corinth walked in incredible anointing and power but was criticized publicly for being carnal (1 Corinthians 3). That church even bestowed membership upon a man who was sleeping with his own mother! They were a people of tremendous gifting but were making poor choices in their character.

The history of the people of God is littered with people who were touched by God but not ultimately changed. Samson was one such person. Endowed with incredible strength and fighting ability, he had the capacity to be a hero for the mature; however, the flaws in his character led him astray. He broke his vows, was sexually indiscreet, and paid a heavy price.

Solomon was another man who was touched by God but not changed. He had great favor, wisdom, and the manifest presence of God in his life. He squandered everything that he had been given and became a disillusioned man with outrageous appetites.

Wolves in Sheep's Clothing

In Matthew 7:15–23, Jesus described what people with these kinds of character flaws are like.

> *Beware of the false prophets, who come to you in sheep's clothing, but inwardly are ravenous wolves. You will know them by their fruits. Grapes are not gathered from thorn bushes nor figs from thistles, are they? So every good tree bears good fruit, but the bad tree bears bad fruit. A good tree cannot produce bad fruit, nor can a bad tree produce good fruit. Every tree that does not bear good fruit is cut down and thrown into the fire. So then, you will know them by their fruits.*
>
> *Not everyone who says to Me, "Lord, Lord," will enter the kingdom of heaven, but he who does the will of My Father who is in heaven will enter. Many will say to Me on that day, "Lord, Lord, did we not prophesy in Your name, and in Your name cast out demons, and in Your name*

perform many miracles?" And then I will declare to them, "I never knew you; DEPART FROM ME, YOU WHO PRACTICE LAWLESSNESS."

What we build with our gifting can be destroyed by our character. A person becomes a wolf in sheep's clothing when they continuously ignore accountability for their own life. Character issues begin to go unresolved and they become unteachable and ungovernable. The important thing to God is that we walk as He does. If we walk in His light, He will open the way for us. If we don't, God may very well close a door on us in order to keep us from compounding our sin.

Good leadership enables people to govern themselves. A man who cannot control himself needs to submit to the control of others, even though it is much better if they work through it themselves and come to a place of self-control. An ungovernable person has lost their humility and servant spirit. "How can you question me?" they reply to criticism. "I'm a man of God!" "I'm a prophet of the Lord. How can you doubt my work?" Every situation in life has a lesson in it for us.

We can question these leaders the same way we can question younger believers. The truth is that the experience they have of walking with God should propel them past the character issues that make us question them in the first place. We only ask questions when there is something we are not seeing.

I do not consider this approach to be disrespect. In fact, it is respect of a different kind. I want people to have longevity in ministry. I have had many mentors, and the only reason I'm still around in prophetic ministry thirty years after I started is because they would not let me hide things from them. We used to have a saying that, "God may wink at something but the brethren won't let you get away with anything."

Accountability is best provoked from below. That is, I do not consider it my leaders' job to have to ask me questions about my life and ministry, though I certainly welcome that! Rather I consider it my role to be open and honest about my life, my current struggles, and the direction my ministry is taking. There is therefore a particular sense of responsibility that leaders have in regard to moving in loving confrontation. Sadly I have seen leaders abuse and misuse confidential information for their own purposes.

> *God does not seek to shame us*

Nevertheless, despite my own past experiences of such abuse, I would still continue to trust and desire accountability for myself. The alternative is too horrible to contemplate. It is better to trust, be open, and get killed than to be closed to personal truth and input and to kill others with our own lack of character

To me accountability is very humbling and purifying. No one gets to see God without it. I like the fact that I can be challenged on things, and I need relationships with people who will call me on things that don't sit well with them. No one likes that process but it is absolutely necessary for all of us. I may have been in prophetic ministry for thirty years but I'm still very capable of making mistakes. I'm still learning, thankfully! Thank God I have people around me who still have enough love and respect for me to not let me get away with anything. I need that more now than ever before because the stakes in my ministry are higher than ever.

We must never end up hearing God for everyone but ourselves. I have noticed that many prophets practice projectionism — sometimes I wonder if we all used to work in movie theatres! There is a constant temptation to project what God is saying to us onto someone else. Something hits home with us, but we turn it around and give it to someone else. It is like a prophetic hot potato: God gives it to us but we are desperate to get it out of our hands before the music stops.

A good rule for words of correction is to apply that correction to your own life first. If it does not have any personal application then it is for someone else. If it touches an issue that God is addressing in us, then it needs to stay with us. Always apply those words to yourself first so you can become humble enough to give them to the person you have the burden for.

At other times too it may be important to announce — privately if possible for theirs and your sake — as a precursor to moving in prophecy that: "I have this particular issue in my own life too and I'm seeking to work it through. I believe therefore that I have a significant impartation to bring along with the word itself."

There is a peculiar grace that comes upon such openness and honesty. We can receive a fresh impartation as well as the people we are prophesying over. What you give comes back to you!

God has to break us before He can trust us with a word of warning, correction, or judgment. Broken people give those types of words best because they have cost something in their own life. Harsh words cannot come out of a hard heart and should be given with tears in the eyes.

Many, many years ago, there was a man in my church who I really struggled with. We had a love/hate relationship: I hated to love him, and he loved to hate me. We just could not get along and conflicted in every conceivable way.

One morning, the Lord showed me a sin in the man's life. "Hallelujah," I thought to myself, "today must be my birthday! I'm going to nail this guy once and for all." I grabbed my coat and started walking to his house. I was so happy with this turn of events that I was whistling.

About a hundred yards from his door, God spoke to me again.

"What are you doing?" He asked.

"I'm going to give the word of the Lord!" I replied happily.

"Graham," the Lord said firmly, "if you ring his doorbell, I am finished with your ministry."

In a heartbeat, I had fallen out of being the "right" one, and into sin. I wanted to get into my enemy's face and give him the business, but God wanted something different.

"Lord, what should I do?" I asked quietly.

"That's something you should have asked Me half a mile ago," He said. "Go back home and take your coat off."

I went home, took my coat off, and sat down. I was annoyed, to say the least.

"Now I want you to fast and pray for him," God said. "I want you to keep fasting and praying until your heart is right about this guy."

It took me sixteen days. I still can't believe I was such an idiot. Finally, I got to a place where I didn't want to give him the word. I found it in my heart to pray and bless that man. God broke my heart by showing me things the poor man had suffered over the years. When I got there, the Lord spoke to me again.

"Go and give the word to him," He said.

This time, I didn't want to. I refused to put my coat on. I knelt and prayed and asked God to send someone else.

"Get your coat on or I will discipline you," the Lord said.

I walked as slowly as humanly possible, hoping that God would change His mind. The ten minute walk stretched into more than an hour as I wept over what I had to do. Finally, I knocked on his door.

"What do you want?" he asked.

"I just need to share something with you," I replied. "Can I come in?"

He brought me into the living room where he was having a cup of coffee. He didn't offer me a cup, but it didn't matter anymore. The only thing that mattered was the word I had to give.

"Get on with it," he barked.

I started to cry again.

"What the hell is wrong with you?" he demanded.

"I wish it was anybody other than me sitting here," I said quietly.

"Well, we agree on one thing at least," he snarled.

"A couple of weeks ago, I heard from the Lord about something. I have been praying about it and I want to share it with you." I told him what the Lord had shown me about the sin in his life. He went white as a ghost and fell off his chair, crying.

"I have been fasting the last two weeks," he told me. "I just can't live this way any more. Two weeks ago, I asked the Lord to send someone to help me."

God wasn't only interested in healing the sin. He also wanted to reconcile the two of us in the process. That man became one of my closest friends. I prayed with him, right there in his living room, and he was immediately delivered. He never struggled with that issue again. God miraculously broke his desire for that sin.

God allows us our preferences but not our prejudice

If I had walked into his home as a wolf in sheep's clothing, I would have killed both of us spiritually. But by submitting to the conviction of the Holy Spirit, I gained a dear, lifelong friend and comrade.

It is not always easy to accept correction, but there is a benefit that comes out of it. Having a teachable spirit strengthens who we are and empowers the very relationship in which the correction occurs.

People who continue in blatant sin while exercising supernatural gifts create an ever-widening gulf between their character and ministry. This gulf can result in spiritual failure, emotional collapse, mental breakdown, physical illness, relational difficulties, and, quite often, a complete moral lapse. As that gap grows, we just give the enemy more room to rush in. There are times when that gap actually cries out to us, and if we don't respond with repentance, a spirit of deception can come and take that ground from us. We start to ignore the signs and carry on with this great cancer afflicting our spiritual lives.

The enemy flies around us, looking for a landing strip of unconfessed sin. That sin gives him the legal right to drop any cargo he likes. Supernatural ministry can bring a greater intensity of satanic attack. To be a warrior, we have to pay the price. No one fights for free; it costs us everything. The people Jesus rebuked in Matthew 7 had left their characters open to demonic attack, and they were twisted and deceived into thinking they were doing God's work. It can happen to anyone.

When God begins to lift us into places of revelation and power, we may as well paint a big target on ourselves. The choice is ours: be a target or a victim. I choose to be a target because if I'm a target for the enemy, I must be an even larger target for the Lord to use. I trust God more on the day of trouble than I trust anyone else any time. I expect my life to have trouble because I expect to fight. We're caught up in a global war, with God on one side and the devil on the other, and I want to fight in that battle. I want to fight injustice, sin, carnality, greed, lust, and mediocrity. I want the church to be pure and powerful and passionate.

If you can be corrected, you can be trusted

Personal Healthiness

Revelational prophecy brings correction and direction from God. If we aspire to move in this level of prophetic gifting, we must take phenomenal care of our character. Otherwise, our gifting could destroy the church. I know a man who has given some amazingly eloquent prophetic words but the truth is, since he started speaking into his church, its congregation has shrunk from more than five hundred and fifty to about two hundred and seventy. When you talk to the people who have left, they all talk about this one prophetic individual. All roads lead back to him. What was the fruit of his ministry? He cut his church in half. What kind of fruit is that?

Words of correction are concerned with the morality and purity of the work. That concern must be reflected in our own lives. Disregarding a lifestyle of accountability produces a nature that is ungovernable and untrustworthy.

The stakes are too high to permit people with a non-accountable gifting to speak into the church. The character of any ministry must be open to view and open to comment from mature people. It is an absolute prerequisite. We have to earn the right to prophesy, or preach, or teach into the work. Our leadership responsibility is to guard the flock and set an example of humility and accountability that the church can follow.

We cannot insist that an individual's character be 100 percent right, otherwise no one would be in leadership or ministry. We must, however, insist that there be a framework around his or her life for the development of their character. There must be real progress in this area before people are permitted to move out into the ministry or take responsibility for others.

It is important that we allow others access and the ability to speak into our relationships, marriage, sexuality, finances, parenting, and how we run our homes and ministries. Our open and honest relationships can protect any fertile ground that the enemy wanted to plant in. It is only through the process of accountability that we come into self-government and learn how to police our own lives well.

No discrepancies should exist between who we are on the inside and what we appear to be on the outside. When we narrow those issues down and eliminate them, our rough edges are made smooth. Our motives are in check, and we minister not to further our own fame or profile, but to spread the kingdom of God.

The favor of God works best in difficult circumstances

The critical question facing every ministry is this: "Are you the owner of your ministry, or the steward of it?" To test us in this, God graciously and elegantly prods us. What rises up in us when we do the grunt work and someone else gets the glory for it? What happens in our hearts when a person is put in authority over us? What do we feel when someone asks us to step back from ministry for a season?

If we are stewards of our life and ministry, we recognize that it is God who opens and closes every door. No man can shut a door that the Lord wants open, and no man can open a door that God has closed. A steward lives at peace with what happens around him. They know that God is in firm control. If He is not behind us, it isn't worth doing anyway. Anyone who has been given a spiritual gift or called to ministry will have to settle the question of ownership.

In my ministry, I have faced opposition many times. Men have tried to deny me things, but I just let it happen. I don't want to fight a war with anyone on earth. I trust the Lord to do the right thing when people do the wrong thing. At the end of the day, I live my life for an audience of One, and if He is unhappy with my ministry, I have bigger issues than what any human being can create for me. I trust Him on days when I seem to have tons of favor and on days when I seem to have none. When we seek and receive God's favor, everything falls into place around us.

Everyone's life gives evidence of what they believe to be true

It is an eloquent test of His Lordship when we are denied opportunity to speak or move in ministry. What are we going to do? How will we respond? This is the best moment to discover the extent of your current favor. Take it to the Lord in prayer and trust His majesty. Learn peace and patience.

The alternative is that we complain, get offended, and possibly become critical and divisive, thus proving that the decision was correct!

Possibly the Lord may be pruning our gift: closing our mouth in order to open our heart so that He may take us to a new depth of compassion and grace for people. The decision to curtail our ministry may be unjust. This would be a very good time to grow patience and also long-suffering with joy! Possibly the Lord wants to further develop your prophetic call through the private ministry of intercession.

Some prophetic seasons must be spent praying before the throne over prophetic input you have received. To pray in a prophetic word rather than speak it out publicly is just as valid, powerful, and anointed. All things work together for good. What is the Lord teaching you through this particular scenario?

When public ministry is denied us, it is our opportunity to develop a private practice with God in throne room prayer. We must become governable in our private lives. What we do publicly in meetings often has very little to do with our actual lives and lifestyles. Meetings are the least important part of church life. They are valuable, but ultimately not as important as Christians make them out to be. What is going on in our homes is of greater consequence. That is where the kingdom of heaven is established or not and where the reality of the lordship of Jesus is seen. Our public face is almost irrelevant.

Prophetic ministry becomes very difficult if we lose our servant spirit in the work because it results in us hearing God for everyone else, but not ourselves. Accurate revelation does not equal godly character. Just because I prophesy over people and hit the mark every time, it does not mean that I am absolutely wonderful in my private life back home. The two do not equal each other, and we must not fall into the trap of thinking that they do. Things are not okay just because someone receives revelation.

We need to be so careful with people in the area of character. We have a right to insist that a certain level of character be demonstrated in people's lives before we turn them loose into any kind of ministry or leadership. If we see someone with gifting and ministry emerging, we have to be prepared to shape their character and lifestyle.

In Vacaville, character is such an important value that I have an action plan for all the people I am discipling. Each of them has specific goals in terms of their marriage, family, relationship with God, gifting, vision, burden, ministry, and so on.

Several years ago, one of the people I was working with in another church had a few severe lifestyle issues that needed to be dealt with. He was simply not responding to the Holy Spirit in those parts of his life. In the end, I had no other choice but to ask him to step back from public ministry for his, and the church's, sake.

It is impossible to keep secrets in church, as there are just too many discerning, mature people in the seats every week. A lot of those Christians knew he was struggling in areas, so we could not release him into public ministry. He fought our request, and I understood that resistance.

"Why can't you be gracious and let me continue while I work through this thing?" he asked.

"That's what we have been doing for the past three months," I replied. "We're at a point now where our grace has to take a slightly different turn, and get a little bit tougher. I'm not enjoying this any more than you are, but for the sake of what we're building, I have to ask you to stop the public life so that you can fix your private life. As soon as you're ready, I want you back in there. I'm not denying you anything. You are denying yourself. You are responsible for your own life, and I need you to take that responsibility."

How did God back me up in this? Well, He gave this man a major prophetic word for the church. Thanks a lot, Lord, I thought when he told me the word. Out of respect for him, I listened, took it away, and weighed it before the Lord. God confirmed it, so I went back to him and said that I felt it was the word of the Lord as well.

When you lose your integrity, you're lost

"Great," he said. "When am I going to give it?"

"You're not," I answered. In the days that followed, God and I had some long conversations about the timing of the word.

"Why now?" I asked Him. "You and I agreed he needed discipline, and I took all of the necessary steps, and this is how You thank me? By giving him this major word?"

"Correct Me if I'm wrong, Graham," the Lord replied, "but I thought you were praying for a way to get deeper into this guy's heart." I went back to the man and reaffirmed my commitment to him and his ministry.

"Everything in me wants to see you succeed," I said. "I want you to be the best you can be for Jesus. I respect your ministry, and your life up to a point. But beyond that point, I just can't. Still, I believe this to be the word of the Lord so I want to work with you."

Over the next few weeks, we worked on the word. He helped me in the judging and weighing process. We talked about the word's implications and strategies. I included him in everything, but I never let him give the word.

We called a church meeting to deliver the word. The man was there with me, but I was the one who got up to speak.

"We received a word a while ago that I'm going to give this evening. The person who gave us the word is so-and-so. We've worked through it, and I've really enjoyed working with him and getting to know him better. I'm going to give his word as he gave it to me."

I honored him for his gift, but I did not allow him to own that word. I found a way of honoring him so everyone would value and appreciate him, but the principle of discipline was still present. In the weeks following that meeting, he broke through his issues. We were able to return him to public ministry. It broke his stubborn independence and taught him the value of relationship.

The One who knows us best loves us best!

Immature people need public restraint and private development. It is not enough to police people, we have to teach them self-control. The best person to police us is ourselves. If we exercise control over ourselves, no one else has to. The only form of human control acceptable to Christ is self-control. None of us are called to rule anyone else's life. Instead, we are called to teach them how to govern themselves. In James 3:17–18, we are given some good advice about character: "*But the wisdom from above is first pure, then peaceable, gentle, reasonable, full of mercy and good fruits, unwavering, without hypocrisy. And the seed whose fruit is righteousness is sown in peace by those who make peace.*"

In this passage, wisdom from above includes revelatory prophecy. It is clear that the things that proceed form God's heart are to be pure. They should have no tinge of humanity to them and should be pure in motive. It would be impure to give a prophetic word which benefits ourselves. It is impure to mix our own opinion into a prophetic word. It is absolutely vital that when there is tension between people, any prophecy given must be completely impartial.

To get to that level of purity, we have to cleanse ourselves. In times of difficulty, my best advice is to get away for three days to fast and pray. Waiting on God cleanses us and helps us to hear a pure word from the Lord.

If we don't have a word from God for a difficult situation, we must keep our mouths shut. Our only role in a time like that is to pray and intercede. When we get drawn into an argument, we disqualify ourselves from hearing God for that situation. After all, how could anyone trust what we are hearing? I would rather pray twenty-four hours a day than get drawn into an argument. Someone has to represent the Most High, and allow His peace, love, and gentleness to flow.

All prophecy begins a process. It heralds something that is to come. A process is a series of steps that take us from where we are now to the next place of God's intentionality. It is therefore intrinsic in every prophecy and promise that their fulfillment is preceded by a period of adjustment, preparation, and realignment.

If the process is not developed through our relationship with the Lord, then the promise or prophecy may be held up in terms of fulfillment.

Also the Lord seldom mentions how something may occur. We do not know the means by which a prophecy may come to pass. David was given a prophecy about being king that contained nothing about him being chased around the wilderness by a megalomaniac or hiding out in caves with a bunch of malcontents! Joseph's dream about one day ruling over his family contained nothing about slavery and false imprisonment. The word of God is always likened to seed. It must go through a process of development in us before it can bear fruit.

> *And He was saying, "The kingdom of God is like a man who casts seed upon the soil; and he goes to bed at night and gets up by day, and the seed sprouts and grows — how, he himself does not know. The soil produces crops by itself; first the blade, then the head, then the mature grain in the head. But when the crop permits, he immediately puts in the sickle, because the harvest has come." (Mark 4:26–29)*

Mature counsel is needed regarding the process we must enter into to prepare ourselves. This is a rich part of the discipleship model that we must employ if we are to mentor people into maturity. We either have assumed or defined relationships as well as understandings regarding how a promise may develop. The Lord may provide definition about the process that helps us to determine our response. If He is vague about the process or provides us no input, then His usual requirement is that we walk closely with Him and develop sensitivity. In the soil of our circumstances, our intimacy with the Lord will enable us to stay on track so that we come into the place and season of fruitfulness.

> *"Listen to this! Behold, the sower went out to sow; as he was sowing, some seed fell beside the road, and the birds came and ate it up. Other seed fell on the rocky ground where it did not have much soil; and immediately it sprang up because it had no depth of soil. And after the sun had risen, it was scorched; and because it had no root, it withered away. Other seed fell among the thorns, and the thorns came up and choked it, and it yielded no crop. Other seeds fell into the good soil, and as they grew up and increased, they yielded a crop and produced thirty, sixty, and a hundredfold." And He was saying, "He who has ears to hear, let him hear!" (Mark 4:3–9)*

Take the prophecy as a seed and ask for help in the current soil of your situation. How do you avoid becoming hard? How can you prevent yourself from being robbed by the enemy? What issues of life may develop anxiety, unbelief, and ungodly desires that will steal your focus on becoming aligned with the Lord and His purpose for you? Are there any challenges, difficulties or persecution that will cause you to lose faith and impetus in your current walk with the Lord?

Every prophecy needs ongoing preparation and focus in order for it to be fulfilled in the season of God's choosing. The purpose of a good mentor is to ask questions, not just to answer them. It is so important that we allow ourselves to be challenged to think and respond to the claims of God in Christ.

Conclusion

I do not want to be known for my gifting or my ministry or my books or my words; I want to be known for who I am in Jesus. One of the reasons I am not afraid to tell a story that makes me look bad is because I do not want anyone to have a false idea about me. I am very, very human. I am not the finished product by any stretch of the imagination. I am on the same journey as every other man and woman is, and I aspire to be something greater than I am today. The only lovable thing about me is what Jesus has put in me.

The reason why we have these guidelines for handling revelatory prophecy is to keep our gift under control. These protocols are a way to build relationship with the people around us. Going to my friends with a word, and relying on their help to judge and weigh it, connects us. It gives us all an equal stake in what God wants to do next.

I cannot overstate how important mutual submission is in prophecy. At the end of the day, we all serve each other. I want the people in my church to succeed. I want them to be spiritually vibrant, financially prosperous, relationally motivated, and generously caring. My success is less important than theirs.

"*But examine everything carefully; hold fast to that which is good,*" Paul wrote in 1 Thessalonians 5:21. We must inspect the fruit of people with supernatural gifting, both in terms of ministry and character. Even more importantly, we need to inspect our own fruit. Our ministries have to be open to being tried and proved. Even our good track record needs watching. We must not get complacent about the ministry. I expect my ministry to be tried and proved until the day I die, and I would not have it any other way.

Notes

Notes

Notes

Guidelines For Handling Prophecy

Reflections, Exercises and Assignments

The following exercises are designed with this particular chapter in mind. Please work through them carefully before going on to the next chapter. Take time to reflect on your life journey as well as your prophetic development. Learn to work well with the Holy Spirit and people that God has put around you so that you will grow in grace, humility, and wisdom in the ways of God.

Graham Cooke.

What Constitutes Maturity?

Prophetic maturity is concerned with displaying sound wisdom and knowledge alongside good practice and accountable, teachable behavior. It is connected to the development of Christlike characteristics and demonstrating the values and temperament of the Holy Spirit. Within the context of this chapter you must be willing and able to develop these attributes as a sign of your growing maturity.

- Being able to move on from a purely spontaneous style of prophecy to something more measured, articulate, anointed and crafted. Thereby having a greater impact on the lives of people.
- Actively seeking a level of openness and honesty regarding your own lifestyle, with friends and leaders around you. Asking for advice and help with struggles you are facing.
- Loving the learning in every situation you encounter! In order to develop a commitment to the Lord we must become committed to our own development in the Spirit.
- Changing your methodology in how you receive, work with, and deliver a prophetic word.
- Being able to define and articulate the process that the Holy Spirit is using to train and develop both character and gift in your daily life.
- Developing partnerships in ministry that have real worth and value both for your relationships and your ministry.
- Cultivating interactive relationships with the prophetic gifts of other people. Knowing how your gifting complements the gifts of other team members.
- Applying the principles of revelation, interpretation, and application in a consistent and responsible manner. This is where you learn to become trustworthy and respected.
- Discover your own credibility gap between your gift and character. Enlist mentoring and support to close that gap as quickly and effectively as possible.
- Exploring and utilizing an intercessory capacity alongside your prophetic gifting. Time spent in throne room prayer is the foundation for prophetic longevity.

What Constitutes Immaturity?

Immaturity develops through a constant failure to learn the lessons of life and spirituality. Bluntly, we are tested on everything we are taught. Grace comforts us when we fail the test; truth prepares our hearts to take it again. When carnality does not decrease, wisdom does not grow and we are challenged again to put on Christ.

If we are dishonest about what we are learning we will only react to events and people rather than respond to the Living God. It is one thing to trust the Lord, it is quite another to be trusted by Him! Within the context of this chapter you must face up to the challenges of ongoing immaturity. Here are the possibilities for your consideration.

- Failure to develop an ongoing relationship and ministry partnership with your leadership.
- Not demonstrating a teachable spirit and defaulting on your ability and willingness to learn. If you can only be corrected through confrontation and conflict, then you have the larger problem of being un-Christlike.
- Demonstrating a negligence at establishing an accountable lifestyle. If people have to take initiative with you regarding your accountability, you prove your immaturity.
- Moving out of frustration and creating tension in your relationships, not just through your gifting but also your lifestyle. Not moving in love, joy, and peace as part of your relationship with the Holy Spirit.
- Failure to develop a greater sensitivity to the Spirit, people, and the church. Can people hear Jesus when you prophesy?
- Not applying the principles you've learned in team dynamics, and not changing your methods to comply with fresh revelation and good practice.
- Having a visible gap between your character and your gifting and not working to close it!

ASSIGNMENT ONE

Think of a person around your life at this time — particularly someone who is tired, worn out, and feeling downhearted. Read and meditate on Matthew 11:28–30 both for yourself and also for that individual.

Ask the Lord to touch your own life with these words. Ask the Holy Spirit to renew your own heart and mind so that you are strengthened and refreshed. Weariness and being heavy laden are not caused by circumstances but by our internal attitude and mindset. The way that we approach life events will either cause us to triumph or be defeated. Wrong choices cause emotional, mental, and spiritual exhaustion. A continuous habit of experiencing such negative responses will bring us to a place of breakdown where we are overwhelmed. Not just by our circumstances but also by the weight of our accumulated poor choices.

Prophecy goes right to the root of the matter which is the internal approach that we generate in all situations. As a man thinks in his heart, so is he in life. We can only change a mindset with a mindset. Study this passage, think deeply on its meaning, purpose and promise.

With your friend in mind prepare your heart to receive encouragement by answering the following questions.

1. What can you say that would get their eyes off themselves and cause them to see God?

2. What is the Lord's burden for this person?

3. What would your objective be in releasing particular encouragement?

4. Be still and listen to the Lord's heartbeat.

5. Write down key words and phrases relating to specific encouragement and pray over them.

6. What particular promises is the Father releasing to them at this time?

7. Write out a specific word of encouragement that would stimulate their faith and cause them to be inspired.

8. How would you give such a word verbally?

9. Ask the Holy Spirit to speak through you to accomplish His purpose.

10. Give the word verbally; pray and seal it into their heart and hand them the written word also.

ASSIGNMENT TWO

Love – Fruit of the Spirit

Many longtime Christians can name off the Galatians 5 fruit of the Spirit with little or no effort: "Love, joy, peace, patience, kindness, goodness, faithfulness, gentleness, and self-control." But the apostle Paul didn't include the fruit in his epistle to be a memory exercise — he included them as a challenge to believers to become more and more like the Christ they love.

One can almost picture the Holy Spirit showing Paul a tree and whispering in his ear: "People who love Me are like a mighty and fruitful tree. They produce good, godly things on their branches. The fruit of the Spirit is ..." Throughout this prophetic series, we will examine the nine fruit of the Spirit and include exercises on making them more real and visible in our lives. This is the very foundation of strong character which, in turn, is the root of responsible and dynamic prophetic ministry.

The first fruit mentioned in Galatians 5:22–23 is love. Love is a core desire of every human being who has ever walked the earth. We all want to love, and be loved. Think of the thousands of songs, poems, and stories that have been written throughout history on the theme of love. Love is central to everything we do.

Spiritual life is no different. We were created to love God, and for Him to love us. On our best day, He loves us. On our worst day, He loves exactly the same. That's unconditional love in its purest, most wondrous form. In turn, we are to reflect God's love to the people around. "Love your neighbor," Jesus taught. "Love your enemies."

In 1 Corinthians 13:4–8, Paul went to great lengths to describe the kind of love Christians are called to.

> *Love is patient, love is kind and is not jealous; love does not brag and is not arrogant, does not act unbecomingly; it does not seek its own, is not provoked, does not take into account a wrong suffered, does not rejoice in unrighteousness, but rejoices with the truth; bears all things, believes all things, hopes all things, endures all things. Love never fails.*

Most of us have a few of those suggestions down pat, but no one functions fully in all of them. We can always improve the way we love by asking God to give us more opportunities to try to be like Him.

In your journal, list the people who you are having trouble loving right now. What character trait is preventing you from fully loving them? What is bothering you? Chances are God is using that person as a "grace-grower" in your life: He is more interested in how you respond to that individual than in what you want to see change in them. God is always more concerned about us and the condition of our heart than with our complaints about other people. Ask Him to show you more of the spiritual beauty He sees in those people.

Below are fifteen principles from Paul's message on love in 1 Corinthians 13. Which ones are God challenging you on? What is He highlighting to you? Are there specific situations where you know you need to practice the kind of love described? Pray about these themes and mark in your journals the ones you want to work on. Be warned, however: God will test you on the types of love you write down, and He will bring people into your life to grow that grace and discipline.

- Love is patient.
- Love is kind.
- Love is not jealous.
- Love does not brag.
- Love is not arrogant or unbearable.
- Love does not seek its own (it's generous).
- Love is not provoked (it doesn't get angry).
- Love does not take into account a wrong suffered.
- Love does not rejoice in unrighteousness (it doesn't like sin).
- Love rejoices with the truth.
- Love bears all things.
- Love believes all things.
- Love hopes all things.
- Love endures all things.
- Love never fails.

On the following page are some useful questions to consider. Please take time to answer them as thoroughly and honestly as possible. The very presence of God in your life may depend on it!

1. How does this particular aspect of God's nature most inspire you in your relationship with Him?

2. What current circumstances is God using to promote this particular fruit in your life?

3. How is He using this fruit of the Spirit?

4. How will you cooperate with God in this regard?

5. What must change in you?

6. What is the life lesson that you would pass onto others from this particular situation?

CASE STUDY

Matching prophetic delivery with content

The delivery of a prophetic word must match its content. One cannot shout into a person's face that the Lord is giving them rest and peace. Likewise, a prophecy about courage and warrior strength cannot be delivered in a nervous stutter! The context (i.e., the way that you speak the prophecy) must match the content (i.e., the actual word being released). Study the following prophecy and answer the questions following it:

> *John, I see you and a bunch of people on a rubber raft going through white water. There is a high wind and rough water. One person has already gone overboard. Several others are grim-faced, holding onto the ropes, not attempting to paddle or help in any way. Two people have their eyes closed. A couple of others are attempting to paddle but are looking worried.*
>
> *You are on your knees at the front of the boat. Only your paddle is in the water. There is a huge grin on your face. You are clearly reveling in the situation as you apply the paddle to the water.*
>
> *You are coming into a season where the next stage of your journey is going to be anything but smooth. In some ways it could appear to be a rough time but the Lord is going to give you a whole new mindset and approach to this time of difficulty.*
>
> *First, you will not fail, nor be overturned by your situation. You will win through into a place of peace and rest.*
>
> *Second, the Father is giving you a set of circumstances to accelerate your relationship with Him into a whole new place of faith and vision.*
>
> *Some of the people with you will jump ship. Others will be a liability and very unhelpful. Some will want to help, but their capacity to worry or be overly concerned will be a drain on the group's resources.*
>
> *This is about you learning that one person with God is always in the majority, no matter how many are against you. This is about you coming into a place of experiencing the joy of the Lord and receiving power to overcome. There are so many things that God is going to be for you and also specific things He is going to give you at this time.*

Answer the following questions:

1. What is the crux of this word?

2. What is the objective that God has in mind?

3. Notice that the prophecy is unfinished.
    a. What does God want to be for John?

    b. What specific things will the Lord give to John in this situation?

4. What is the outcome that the Lord will guarantee?

5. What is the best way to speak this prophecy?

6. After giving the word, what would you pray over John that would release faith to him?

LECTIO DIVINA

Lectio Divina (Latin for *divine reading*) is an ancient way of reading the Bible, allowing a quiet and contemplative way of coming to God's Word. *Lectio Divina* opens the pulse of the Scripture, helping readers dig far deeper into the Word than normally happens in a quick glance-over.

In this exercise, we will look at a portion of Scripture and use a modified *Lectio Divina* technique to engage it. This technique can be used on any piece of Scripture. I highly recommend using it for key Bible passages that the Lord has highlighted for you, and for anything you think might be an inheritance word for your life (see the Crafted Prayer interactive journal for more on inheritance words).

Read the Scripture:

> *Consider it all joy, my brethren, when you encounter various trials, knowing that the testing of your faith produces endurance. And let endurance have its perfect result, so that you may be perfect and complete, lacking in nothing. But if any of you lacks wisdom, let him ask of God, who gives to all generously and without reproach, and it will be given to him. But he must ask in faith without any doubting, for the one who doubts is like the surf of the sea, driven and tossed by the wind.*
>
> *For that man ought not to expect that he will receive anything from the Lord, being a double-minded man, unstable in all his ways. But the brother of humble circumstances is to glory in his high position; and the rich man is to glory in his humiliation, because like flowering grass he will pass away. For the sun rises with a scorching wind and withers the grass; and its flower falls off and the beauty of its appearance is destroyed; so too the rich man in the midst of his pursuits will fade away.*
>
> *Blessed is a man who perseveres under trial; for once he has been approved, he will receive the crown of life which the Lord has promised to those who love Him. Let no one say when he is tempted, "I am being tempted by God"; for God cannot be tempted by evil, and He Himself does not tempt anyone. But each one is tempted when he is carried away and enticed by his own lust. Then when lust has conceived, it gives birth to sin; and when sin is accomplished, it brings forth death.*
>
> *Do not be deceived, my beloved brethren. Every good thing given and every perfect gift is from above, coming down from the Father of lights, with whom there is no variation or shifting shadow. In the exercise of His will He brought us forth by the word of truth, so that we would be a kind of first fruits among His creatures. This you know, my beloved*

brethren. But everyone must be quick to hear, slow to speak and slow to anger; for the anger of man does not achieve the righteousness of God. Therefore, putting aside all filthiness and all that remains of wickedness, in humility receive the word implanted, which is able to save your souls.

But prove yourselves doers of the word, and not merely hearers who delude themselves. For if anyone is a hearer of the word and not a doer, he is like a man who looks at his natural face in a mirror; for once he has looked at himself and gone away, he has immediately forgotten what kind of person he was.

But one who looks intently at the perfect law, the law of liberty, and abides by it, not having become a forgetful hearer but an effectual doer, this man will be blessed in what he does. If anyone thinks himself to be religious, and yet does not bridle his tongue but deceives his own heart, this man's religion is worthless. Pure and undefiled religion in the sight of our God and Father is this: to visit orphans and widows in their distress, and to keep oneself unstained by the world. (James 1:2–27)

1. Find a place of stillness before God. Embrace His peace. Chase the nattering thoughts out of your mind. Calm your body. Breathe slowly. Inhale. Exhale. Inhale. Exhale. Clear yourself of the distractions of life. Whisper the word, "Stillness." Take your time. When you find that rest in the Lord, enjoy it. Worship Him in it. Be with Him there.

2. Reread the passage twice. Allow its words to become familiar to you. Investigate James's advice on testing. What images does that bring to your spirit? What do you see? Become a part of it. What phrases or words especially resonate with you? Meditate especially on those shreds of revelation. Write those pieces down in your journal.

3. Read the passage twice again. Like waves crashing onto a shore, let the words of Scripture crash onto your spirit. What excites you? What scares you? What exhilarates you about this revelation of the nature of God? What are you discerning? What are you feeling? What are you hearing? Again, write it all down in your journal.

4. Write the theme of this passage in your journal.

5. Does this passage rekindle any memories or experiences? Does it remind you of any prophetic words you have given or received? Write those down as well.

6. What is the Holy Spirit saying to you through this Scripture? Investigate it with Him — picture the two of you walking through it together. Write those words in your journal.

7. Read the passage two final times. Meditate on it. Is there something God wants you to do? Is there something He is calling you to? Write it down.

8. Pray silently. Tell God what this passage is saying to you. Tell Him what you are thinking about. Write down your conversation together. Picture yourself and the Holy Spirit as two old friends in a coffee shop, chatting about what God is doing.

9. Finally, pray and thank God for His relationship with you. Come back to the passage once a week for the next three months. Read it and let more revelation flow into you. If you feel compelled to, craft a prayer based on this passage for yourself, your family, your friends, or your church. Pray that prayer until you feel God has birthed it in you.

Notes

Notes

Notes

Notes

Notes

MODULE TWO

EVALUATING THE PROPHETIC WORD

MODULE TWO

Evaluating the Prophetic Word

WHAT YOU WILL LEARN IN THIS SEGMENT:

- The difference between Old and New Testament prophets.
- Accountability as a lifestyle.
- All prophecy must be tested and weighed.
- The biblical pattern for prophecy.
- Edification, exhortation and comfort…the antidote to negativity.
- How to work with negative impressions.
- The prophetic role is to build and plant.
- Purpose of godly authority.
- How to test the spirit behind the prophecy.
- The true nature of the gift of discerning of spirits.
- Accuracy is not the prime test of authenticity.
- Aligning prophecy and Scripture.
- Neither God nor prophecy are wholly logical.
- The prime purpose of a prophet is to glorify Jesus.
- The signs of manipulation and control.
- Prophecy and the will of the individual.
- Soul ties, good and bad.
- Avoiding exclusivity and being super spiritual.
- Do not make yourself an oracle.
- The importance of good feedback.
- Prophecy is often paradoxical.
- Prophecy must contend with people for what God intends.

MODULE TWO

Evaluating the Prophetic Word

WHAT YOU WILL LEARN IN THIS SEGMENT:

- A servant spirit is at the heart of all ministry.
- The importance of establishing a good track record in the prophetic gift.
- Learn to appreciate that one of the main roles of leadership is to protect the flock.
- Know the difference between false prophecy and poor prophecy.
- Learn meekness with boldness.
- Continuously update your language and methodology in prophecy so that you remain contemporary.
- Learn to craft prophecy as well as being spontaneous.
- Develop the ability to apply the tests to your own word first, so that the Holy Spirit may adjust you personally.
- Cultivate the aptitude to focus on outcomes so that your content and delivery match the objectives of the Holy Spirit.
- Generate a specific desire to glorify the Lord at all times.
- Be careful that your prophecy is not divisive or judgmental.
- Do not allow yourself to become frustrated but keep your heart pure before the Lord.
- Understand that there are several types of words, each of which has a specific application. Learn them well.
- Make sure that you always have permission from the Lord to speak His heart.
- Learn that sometimes we don't speak prophetically to man but we use the word to intercede to the Lord.

CHAPTER TWO

Evaluating the Prophetic Word

IN THE NEW TESTAMENT CHURCH, prophecy occurs on a different level than what existed in the Old Testament. John the Baptist was the last of the Old Testament prophets, and Jesus the first in a new line of New Testament prophets.

Life for a prophet in the old covenant was very difficult. In those days, prophets were sometimes a single voice speaking God's word to a corrupt and rebellious nation. They were often persecuted and derided for their words. They lived lives of immense hardship. Daniel was thrown into a lion's den. Samson had his eyes plucked out. Samuel was forced into giving Israel a king. Elijah and Elisha were hounded by the authorities. Joseph was sold into slavery.

Prophets are team players

And then there was Ezekiel. He was told at an early age that he was being sent to a people who would not listen to him. At the beginning of his ministry, God told him that his forehead would have to be like flint (Ezekiel 3:9) in order for him to survive. All of his life, he contended with the rebellious nature of God's people. His call was to prophesy, whether the people listened to him or not (Ezekiel 3:11). Not exactly an exciting job description!

New Testament prophecy, modeled by Jesus Himself, changed much of that. While some things are the same between the two covenants, the new model incorporates prophets into the body of Christ. A prophet is a member of that body like any other Christian. Therefore, a prophet is obliged to function in fellowship and cooperation with other parts of the body. This places certain restrictions on us that are good for the ministry and the church.

As fellow members of the body of Christ, we have a right to insist that the prophetic ministries that visit us are accountable for what they do. One of the biggest problems in the church today is the number of prophetic ministries who spend hardly any time in a home church. These itinerant ministers are away too many weeks a year and lose the ability to have meaningful, accountable relationships with a particular body of people. Every weekend, they speak at another conference or in someone else's church. I have found that this kind of schedule and life damages the revelation they receive as they are unable to work long-term through the tension that arises from any prophetic word.

When prophetic ministries come to speak, the local church has the right to ask some hard questions.

- Are you rooted in a local church?
- Are you accountable to that leadership?
- What is the fruit from your ministry there?
- Who takes responsibility for your ministry and giftings while you are away from home?
- What redress have we got if things go wrong?

We cannot allow unaccountable people to come into our work and speak the word of God when no one is speaking it into their own lives. This level of accountability should not just exist for a prophet; itinerant evangelists, teachers, pastors, and apostles should all have to answer these hard questions.

Accountability is best provoked from below rather than imposed from above. Everyone should be requiring and requesting accountable relationships as part of the lifestyle of community within the kingdom of God.

If accountability is imposed from above it often ceases to be relational. We police people rather than teach them self-control and personal government. We devise a system of rewards and punishments to keep people in check because we're mostly only concerned about functional liabilities, rather than preparing people for an ongoing personal encounter with a loving, gracious, and firm God.

To be wholly accountable to others we need to set people free to use their will properly. Everyone has freedom to choose. Wise choices in life are a hallmark of maturity.

Accountability if it has to be forced on people will never set them free or create mature believers. Quite the opposite. It will prevent people from understanding the true nature of God.

In real accountable situations we are attempting to primarily confront people with their freedom: "It is for freedom that Christ set us free" (Galatians 5:1). Leaders do not parent the flock, they partner with people. The choices people make regarding their dreams and aspirations must lead them into a greater place of self-government and interdependence within the team.

Accountability when not imposed or demanded from above finds its truest grace in the promotion of the individual above the corporate.

People matter more than systems. Most accountability structures in the church are more concerned with control than freedom. Leaders who are more functional than relational build program style churches that do everything for effectiveness and efficiency. The corporate body is deemed more important than the personal, and their accountability structure reflects that approach. As long as people stay within the narrow confines of our behavior code, they have the pastoral OK. A supernatural lifestyle though does not fit into a rigid program blueprint for church. The prophetic is an outside-the-lines voice that causes us to listen to God, be sensitive to the Holy Spirit, and to live by faith rather than logic.

We have systems that are natural and organizationally inspired with sound reasoning behind them. Life in the Spirit is organic not systematic. It is highly supernatural and occurs totally out of an ongoing divine encounter with a Spirit who is God!

Something has to give. It is usually freedom that is curtailed. Easier to punish people rather than disciple them.

For many years, I have been teaching schools of prophecy around the world. In each new place, I have to fight through suspicion, wariness, mistrust, subjective poor experience, and antagonism. In many cases, when I ask questions in return, I discover that I am the first prophet these people have actually encountered. Most bad experiences have occurred during poor body ministry within the life of a church, or from evangelistic, teaching, and itinerant ministries that have moved in the prophetic without proper lines of accountability being established.

Prophets are not some sort of superstar ministry, but a member of the church universal. In all Scripture passages referring to prophetic ministry in the New Testament church, we read about a plurality of prophets. We need to ensure that any strong prophetic figures in our church are relating to others with whom they feel comfortable. Iron sharpens iron, and prophetic people need to be together to sharpen each other within a process that is governed and accountable.

In my own ministry, I have a number of prophetic people, within a variety of churches from across the denominational spectrum, who work with me on schools of prophecy and conferences. This has the blessing and approval of those local churches involved. In a number of cases, I have established prophetic guidelines and practices in those churches and have been instrumental in the Lord redeeming prophetic ministries that had fallen off track.

The implication in Scripture is that an individual prophet is a member of a group and, therefore, has a ministry that is coordinated with others. It is clearly and emphatically stated that all prophecy in a New Testament church is subject to evaluation.

> *"Let two or three prophets speak, and let the others pass judgment."*
> *(1 Corinthians 14:29)*

"Do not quench the Spirit; do not despise prophetic utterances. But examine everything carefully; hold fast to that which is good." (1 Thessalonians 5:19–21)

We cannot be too careful when scrutinizing prophecy. Many words are extremely elaborate and hold long-term implications for our lives and churches.

Therefore, we should follow an exhaustive process to judge and weigh a word. If a prophecy fails to meet any one of these tests, we should reject it, trace it back to its source, and work through the difficulties and anomalies with the people concerned. When evaluating a prophetic word, there are eight main tests to consider.

- What is the biblical pattern?
- Does it edify, exhort, and comfort?
- What is the spirit behind the prophecy?
- Does the prophecy conform to Scripture?
- Does the prophecy glorify Jesus?
- Is it manipulative or controlling? If so, what are the signs of that manipulation and control?
- How do we handle negative prophecy?
- How do we apply the tests?

The goal of accountability is freedom!

Biblical Pattern

In the church today, two extreme schools of thought exist regarding prophecy. Both of them are wrong. One portion of the church rejects prophecy altogether. They believe prophecy belongs to another time and dispensation of God's power. "We don't need prophecy today because we have the Bible," they say. They replace prophecy with teaching, preaching, and Bible study — the only three ways they believe God communicates with the earth. The Bible, it is argued, is the sole means of revelation today. This wing of the church despises prophecy and therefore quenches the Holy Spirit, the very Spirit of prophecy.

The other extreme view is just as wrong. Some Christians accept all prophecy without testing or weighing it. Of course, this is made more difficult by the actions and antics of some so-called prophets locked in a "man of God" syndrome. Their attitude declares, "I am the man of God. You must listen to me." Any venture at accountability, any request for explanation, or any attempt at assessing the prophetic word is seen as an insult to the "man of God's" integrity. I have come across countless cases of local pastors being pressured, intimidated, and subtly bullied into accepting revelation. Many church leaders are not equipped to resist these indirect strong-arm tactics. In prophetic terms, we cannot allow an Old Testament hierarchy to prevail in a New Testament culture.

Prophets cannot pull rank on local church leaders. The fivefold ministries operate under a team concept designed to provide safeguards for the church at large.

The New Testament pattern is to be open to the prophetic gift and give respectful attention to prophetic revelation. We submit each prophecy to careful Scriptural scrutiny and accept only that which passes these tests. Most importantly, we deal with prophecy that doesn't pass muster. We should not let wrong prophecy slide. We must be allowed to go back down the line to ask for redress when a prophecy is dubious. It is the job of the leaders to protect the flock. All credible prophetic ministries will understand that and cooperate with this important part of a pastor's role.

Many leaders feel they cannot approach prophets because it seems as though they are questioning their very credibility. Others sweep the mess under the rug because they know that confronting the prophet may be more trouble than it is worth. Allowing bad prophecy to stand is against New Testament teaching and leads to abuses within the ministry. It discredits the prophetic gift.

I want to emphasize again that people who aspire to be in prophetic ministry must become an established part of a local church. Our ministry must be evident there. It needs to be seen and noted by the other church leaders. Without those roots, we will not understand some of the wider things God wants to do in the church. We'll end up as "seagull prophets," people who fly in, make a loud noise, dump on everyone, and fly out again.

Church leaders should be put at ease by a prophet's behavior. We neither lord over people nor demote ourselves with a subservient spirit. Lines of trust, love, and friendliness should be established within a firm structure of accountability. Local church leaders should feel comfortable with visiting prophets. Likewise, prophets should feel relaxed and not under a microscope to perform.

Every prophet should have an established framework and routine of accountability. Every itinerant minister — and local pastor, for that matter — should be answerable to someone. A prophet operating alone is out of balance. However, a pastor, teacher, evangelist, or apostle, by themselves, is just as out of balance. More errors in doctrine and practice, more control and manipulation, and more lives have been ruined by unaccountable pastors than by faulty prophets. In many churches, the pastor's word is law and cannot be questioned without people being labeled as difficult or rebellious.

We label what we do not love

The answer to misuse is not non-use but proper use. Not throwing the gift away, but instead insisting that it be used properly. Every leader and minister must take it upon himself to establish lines of credibility and integrity. This keeps the church safe.

Although prophecy is supernatural, it is up to us to know how to handle it. In 1 Corinthians 12, the apostle Paul wrote about the gifts of the Spirit. In chapter thirteen, he taught us that love ought to be the basic ingredient behind all supernatural manifestations. First Corinthians 14 explains how to handle the gifts.

Allow prophets to speak, and then follow up with evaluation. Be aware of the dangers of making any adjustments in the life of a church or an individual before the judging process is complete. Separate out what is good by sound, objective testing. Deal with words that do not pass this safety check.

Allowing prophecy without first testing it violates New Testament principles. It produces a shallow experience and often provokes people to view future words with contempt. Unchecked prophecy allows charlatans to grow fat, thrive on our ignorance, and further damage responsible prophetic people and the church itself.

Edification, Exhortation, Comfort

Does the word edify, exhort, and comfort? (1 Corinthians 14:3)

The true purpose of prophecy is to build, admonish, stir up, encourage, release people from their pain and discomfort, and enable us to know and understand the heartbeat of God for ourselves. If a word does not achieve these purposes, it is not true prophecy. If it births confusion, discouragement, or condemnation, it should not be accepted. In fact, in some cases, such a faulty word needs to be clearly and forcefully rejected to prevent a curse from taking hold of someone's life. A thin line separates the gift of prophecy from the evil spirit of divination, and we have to make sure that the people we prophesy over are coming into blessing in God and not into a curse. Prophetic ministries that continually give negative words need ministry and deliverance themselves.

The final purpose of prophecy is always positive. A prophet must bring good news even if that news is... repent! However, some negativity may exist within a word; this is proper and fits within the economy of God. In the end, though, the prophetic word must edify, exhort, and comfort.

When God gives us a negative word, it should be used as a word of knowledge for the prophet to consider. It provides a context for the amazing thing God wants to do. We need not prophesy someone's sin to them as they already know they are flawed. Instead, a negative word should spark us to ask questions of God. What is it He wants us to say and do? What does He want to do for this person? God's objective determines the way we speak the word.

Often, we have to replace a negative in a person's life with a positive. Jeremiah's prophetic ministry is a perfect example of this principle. In Jeremiah 1:10, God commissioned the prophet with this call: "See, I have appointed you this day over the nations and over the kingdoms, to pluck up and to break down, to destroy and to overthrow." Those are four obvious negatives, but God's commission didn't end there. The Father added two positives to the list: "to build and to plant." Sometimes, a prophet has to pull something negative down in order to replace it with a positive. Before something can be built, land has to be cleared. We sometimes need the negative to come out because there are things God wants to root out, pull down, destroy, and throw down before He builds and plants. The first part of a prophecy can be negative, but only if it births something positive in the end.

Anything negative must always be challenged

Our role in the church is to build. We build the kingdom by edifying the people through the ministry of the gospel, the exercise of our spiritual gifts, and the use of biblical leadership. The apostle Paul certainly modeled that building mentality for us. Twice he wrote about his authority from God. In 2 Corinthians 10:8, Paul wrote about "our authority, which the Lord gave for building you up and not for destroying you." Later, in 2 Corinthians 13:10, he explained why he wrote some difficult things to the church in Corinth: "For this reason I am writing these things while absent, so that when present I need not use severity, in accordance with the authority which the Lord gave me for building up and not for tearing down." His authority, therefore, was to build something up, not pull something down.

Although we may have some negative things to prophesy, our whole motivation must be to build the work up. This is the model shown us in 1 Corinthians 14, where Paul instructed us on the proper use of spiritual gifts. Seven times in that chapter he used the word "edification," which means, "to build up." Our prophetic revelation must leave people feeling challenged and blessed.

Test the Spirit

What is the spirit behind the prophecy? (1 John 4:13)

Behind every prophecy there are three possible sources: the Spirit of God, the spirit of man, or an evil spirit. It is vital when judging a prophetic word that we discover the spirit which gave it, as we read in 1 John 4:13:

> *Beloved, do not believe every spirit, but test the spirits to see whether they are from God, because many false prophets have gone out into the world. By this you know the Spirit of God: every spirit that confesses that Jesus Christ has come in the flesh is from God; and every spirit that does not confess Jesus is not from God; this is the spirit of the antichrist, of which you have heard that it is coming, and now is already in the world.*

The gift of discerning of spirits is primarily used to detect the presence of God. All of the spiritual gifts lead us toward God. They radiate from Him, they move toward Him, and they emphasize who He is. In a prophetic context, the gift of discerning of spirits tells us whether the word was inspired by God or not. If it is not God who is speaking, the gift will shift into a second gear to determine whether it was the spirit of man that inspired the word. If the answer is again no, then there is only one option left: an evil spirit.

The "gift of discernment" that we often hear about in church does not actually exist; there is only the gift of the discerning of spirits. Some people think that the gift of discerning of spirits is primarily concerned with the enemy, but that is incorrect. They see evil spirits everywhere when in fact the gift operates to discern where the Spirit of God is. We all have a sense of witness in our spirit. Is this God? We usually know if it is or not. When there is no witness in our spirit that it is God speaking to us, we have a good sign that the prophetic word is probably from a different source.

Always look for signs of God's presence!

Prophecy communicates spirit to spirit, as well as speaking into our minds and intellects. We need to discern the spirit behind the prophecy before we discern the words. At the moment, the church at large does this the wrong way around, putting the content of the word ahead of the spirit behind it. But we must weigh the spirit before the accuracy of the content. Prophecy must line up with Scripture and also the Holy Spirit, because there is a spirit to prophecy.

Accuracy is not more important than discerning the spiritual source. In Acts 16:16–18, Luke recorded an intriguing story about the motives behind a prophetic word.

> *It happened that as we were going to the place of prayer, a slave-girl having a spirit of divination met us, who was bringing her masters much profit by fortune-telling. Following after Paul and us, she kept crying out, saying, "These men are bondservants of the Most High God, who are proclaiming to you the way of salvation."*
>
> *She continued doing this for many days. But Paul was greatly annoyed, and turned and said to the spirit, "I command you in the name of Jesus Christ to come out of her!" And it came out at that very moment.*

The slave girl was 100 percent accurate—in fact, she was practically evangelistic in her prophecy. Paul and his company were servants of God and proclaimed salvation. But the accuracy of the word did not make it truly prophetic. We must test the spirit behind the word. Paul weighed the spirit and was grieved by it. He ignored the accuracy of her statement and cast the demon out.

Accuracy is not a prime test!

How many churches have been led astray by not judging the spirit first? Paul, at that time, was in a multi-religious culture. The girl's words were almost reverential and certainly elevated the Lord to the people who heard her. We cannot fault the accuracy, but this is the enemy at his best: masquerading as an angel of light. The counterfeit will always be close to the real thing, like the tares growing up with the wheat. The enemy has invaded the church with false prophecy, just as he has with false teaching, poor evangelistic presentation of the gospel, and a spirit of independence and rebellion. In churches around the world, things are being said that are 100 percent accurate but, just as with the slave girl, it is not the Spirit of God.

In Mark 1:23–27, Jesus ran up against a similar phenomenon. A demon saw Christ and said, "I know who You are — the Holy One of God!" The demon recognized Him before the disciples did! Jesus, for His part, commanded the spirit to be silent.

The flip side of this principle is that a word can contain some small inaccuracies and still be received in the spirit it was given. If we feel as thought the word is from God, we can examine the content and its accuracy.

During a ministry trip in the Caribbean, I prophesied to a man a picture God gave me. In the picture, he was eight years old. His mother had forbidden him to swim by himself at the beach. Disobeying her one day, he had gotten himself in trouble in deep water. He cried out to God for help. Suddenly, a huge wave came out of nowhere and deposited him back on the beach. Running off home, he told no one about his experience. Twenty years later, the Lord showed me all that had happened, and I was able to encourage him that the Lord had saved his life at that tender age for a purpose. The Holy Spirit then outlined in prophecy what that purpose was to be.

Later, the man came to talk with me. He had a question: the experience had happened just as I had prophesied, but it had occurred when he was seven years old, not eight, as I had said. "Does this invalidate the prophecy?" he asked me.

I explained to him that he needed to judge the word by the Spirit and Scripture, and the interpretation of mature, gifted people with wisdom. A friend, overhearing the conversation, asked him for his correct age at the time of his ocean rescue. He was seven years and eleven months old, or "nearly eight," as he put it. I don't think the Lord would mind me being a month out in terms of detail on that occasion! We can receive the spirit of a word despite one or two anomalies in detail.

Witness to the Spirit

People who get hung up on accuracy and content before weighing the spirit of the word are liable to make huge mistakes. We need to do both. In spiritual things, we understand with our mind but know in our spirit. "*For who among men knows the thoughts of a man except the spirit of the man which is in him? Even so the thoughts of God no one knows except the Spirit of God*," Paul wrote in 1 Corinthians 2:11–12. "*Now we have received, not the spirit of the world, but the Spirit who is from God, so that we may know the things freely given to us by God*." We just know in our knower, as the cliché goes. Sometimes, we cannot even explain it to someone else. There are times when our intuition doesn't make sense but we still need to listen to it.

We must weigh the spirit behind the prophecy. Our own spirit will be a good indicator. The Holy Spirit makes His presence felt by His fruit. Love, joy, and peace will be present when He is moving. Conversely, we can feel uneasy and lacking in peace with some prophetic utterances. The words clash with our spirit and do not readily find a home. This initial witness of the spirit is an important guide as a demonic presence will inevitably make its presence felt.

To be effective in the area of discerning of spirits, we need to understand the following five parts of judging and weighing.

1. It is scriptural and right to judge and weigh prophetic words.
2. No person's ministry is exempt from the evaluation process.
3. It is not disrespectful or disloyal to weigh the words of others.
4. Local leaders, as well as international ministries, are to demonstrate accountable behavior.
5. The judging process is vital because it removes any enemy influence while cementing the purposes of God into our conscious minds.

Conformity to Scripture

Does the prophecy conform to Scripture? (Isaiah 8:20)

Our lives are built on Scripture, not on prophecy. In the event of a clash between a word and the Bible, we must always abandon the prophecy in favour of Scripture, the revealed Word of God. We must be especially careful that the substance of extrabiblical revelation does not contradict the Bible, but is in accord with the revealed message.

Prophecy must not be used to establish previously unheard-of doctrine or practices. It is possible to receive prophetic input that opens a church up to seeking God's word in a particular area. The prophecy acts as a stimulus and a catalyst to receive the revealed Word of Scripture, thus causing a change of practice or a new approach to life in God.

For example, I once prophesied to a man that God was calling him to intercessory prayer. At the time, he had a deep longing to go further in prayer and was quite frustrated at his lack of progress. He had never heard of intercession, but that did not disqualify the word. Through conversation and prayer with him and his leaders, we were able to point him towards some teaching resources that got him started. Intercession was new to him, but not unheard of in the historic, universal church.

This is a subtle minefield, full of devious traps and pitfalls. When in doubt about a word, check it out! Prophecy should never be used to govern the understanding of Scripture. We can get excited and be thankful to God for revelational prophecy. However, the moment we step into teaching, preaching, or matters of doctrine, we need to sharpen our concentration. Scripture is the dominant test of all doctrine and practice.

Some aspects of weighing prophecy against Scripture can be quite straightforward. Whenever prophecy contradicts or challenges Christian doctrine and foundational truth, the prophetic word must be renounced. That much is clear.

On other occasions, it can be difficult to put a true prophecy alongside a particular Scripture. This gray area occurs because there are no specific passages that can be used to weigh the prophetic word. For example: I once gave a prophetic word to the city of Cleveland, Ohio, in America. It was given in private sessions with leaders. We can test the general tone of the word by Scripture but not the specific revelation regarding Cleveland as a city — simply because it is not mentioned in Scripture. We must then do our best to weigh the prophecy against the general context of the Bible. Does the word malign any of the truths we hold dear? Where does faith in this prophecy take us? Does it lead us to the feet of Jesus? Is it causing disruption in the body?

Prophecy stimulates growth

The last question is particularly difficult to work through. What does a prophet do when faced with immense needs in church people who are being governed by a corrupt leadership? How do we bring prophetic words into churches where the chief problem is leadership riding roughshod over the people? Obviously, we can, and should, speak to the leaders in private, but what happens if their hearts aren't changed? Do we opt for a quiet life, safeguarding our reputation, and pursuing a policy of noninterference? How do we keep silent when hearts are being broken all around us?

This is the side of the prophetic coin that very few people understand. It is easy to prophesy in a place where the people's indifference is holding the leadership's God-given vision back. Where the leadership is having a difficult time because of the hardness of the people, the issue is clear both prophetically and scripturally. However, very few prophets have what it takes to stand in the other situation where, if we speak out, bless, and release the people, we will open ourselves to accusations of disruption and be labeled off the wall by the leadership. In most cases where the word of the leader is accepted, the opinion of the prophet is never sought. But it can happen, and a prophet must be willing to pay the price.

Gray areas exist where there are no specific, clear words of Scripture to help us determine whether a prophetic word is right. If I give a word about London, Frankfurt, Chicago, or Vancouver, what Scripture do I weigh it against? None of these places are mentioned in the Bible. This limits our ability to align the prophetic word with Scripture except in a general sense.

We must do all we can to confirm or deny the prophetic by proper use of the Bible. Further complicating matters are situations where prophecy is spoken into an issue where people already feel they have an answer from the

Bible. I once gave a man a word that warned him not to accept a job he was about to be offered. He needed to wait for the Lord to move; I felt strongly that the company he was about to join was unethical in its business practices. His association with it would lead him into a place where he would be asked to do things that conflicted with his walk with God.

Unfortunately, the man had been unemployed for two years, and the entire church had been interceding on his behalf. They saw this job offer as an answer to their prayers. I didn't know any of this history. I had just arrived for a conference and picked him out of the crowd with this prophetic word. The church disagreed with me and even used Scripture to back up their belief that the job offer was God's will. He was encouraged to take the job, and I was told that I had missed it.

A few weeks after taking the job, the man was asked to lie so he could pick up a particular order. These ethical dilemmas continued for some time, wreaking havoc on his health and nervous system. Meanwhile, a job that was within his scope of capabilities came and went while he was out of town on business. It was advertised and snapped up within a week while he was away.

He soon had to quit his job because of the double standards. He was again unemployed. He found it difficult to collect welfare because he had left the job voluntarily. The church mishandled the situation, offering no apology or help. He was left disillusioned, jobless, broke, and alone.

In this case, the church had been praying for months. People had received "words" and Bible verses. When a job was offered to him, people were euphoric — it was a certifiable answer to prayer, they thought. What a victory! Into that mix came my word of warning that seemed to clash with the verses people had received. I said at the time that the verses were correct, but not for that job. They were correct for the second job opportunity, not the first. The prophetic word and the Bible verses were not in conflict, but the timing differed.

Something spiritual may not be reasonable

The prophetic input I gave was judged solely on the basis that the church had received Scripture. My word clashed with theirs and they felt they had been praying long enough and that an answer had been given. But anyone familiar with intercession knows that the final furlong of a situation is always the most dangerous. Issues will seem to be on the way to being resolved, and our vigilance and concentration lets up as a result.

In warfare, prayer, and intercession, a period of vulnerability usually exists just before the end. Perseverance is needed to maintain our focus right to the full resolution. As they say in football, always play to the final whistle. Let God, not the circumstances, be the guide. The enemy sometimes makes one last-ditch effort to derail everything before he gives up ground. We can lose a race within sight of the finish line.

Another important rule of thumb is to remember that just because a word is offbeat, it doesn't make it anti-biblical. People have often come to me and said a word I have given them makes no sense to them.

"What makes you think it should?" I answer.

"Well, it just doesn't logically compute," they sometimes say.

"I guess God is just being illogical then," I reply. Much of what God said and did in Scripture is illogical and doesn't make human sense. If our goal is to be logical, we may miss an opportunity to be spiritual and thereby determine the heart of God.

Scripture is full of God's illogical answers to difficult problems. We would have sent the greatest army in the world to free Israel from Egypt, but God sent a stuttering shepherd with a stick and some plagues. We would have sent the greatest soldier in the world to fight Goliath, but God sent a teenager with a slingshot and five shiny stones. We would have chosen the mightiest man in Israel to fight the Midianites, but God chose a kid cowering in a winepress. Only God would choose an army by virtue of how they drank out of a river. It makes no logical sense at all!

God waited until the Israelites had crossed the Jordan into the Promised Land, until they were surrounded by giants and hostile kings, before springing the idea of circumcision on them. Some army! They were all walking like John Wayne for three weeks. They were completely vulnerable, but God was secure in the fact that He could protect them. Only God could defeat Jericho, the most fortified city on the planet, by sending people around it silently for a week, and then, on day seven, having them shout. If a prophet gave a word like that today, we would commit them to an institution. And yet it aligns perfectly with Scripture.

Some prophecies are not meant to make sense. What they are supposed to do is get us thinking, praying, and asking God questions. It is easy to put illogical prophecies on the back burner, but God calls us to explore His will.

Jesus Alone

Does the prophecy glorify Jesus? (1 Corinthians 12:3)

The prime ministry of the Holy Spirit is to bring glory to Jesus: *"He will glorify Me, for He will take of Mine and will disclose it to you,"* says John 16:14. Any prophetic utterance, dream, or vision should accomplish that aim.

Any word that exalts a man's ministry at the expense of the glory of Jesus is unworthy. True prophetic ministry should also teach us how to hear God for ourselves. In this way, we do not create any sense of dependency upon the ministry of the prophet.

Many people are often severely disappointed when they attend a meeting with a prophet and do not receive a word or insight. When this happens, they need to check their own motive: do they hope more in a man or woman's ministry than they do in God?

All of the fivefold ministries are given so that the wider body of Christ may be equipped to do the work of the kingdom. The pastor equips people not just to be released through counseling, but to be able to counsel others. The teacher expounds the Word of God but also releases people to search the Scriptures for themselves. The evangelist not only handles missions and revivals to the unsaved, but also equips the body to do the work of evangelism. The apostle builds up and establishes the body of Christ and releases people into a process of self-government and church planting.

True prophecy is the intent of the Father

In a similar vein, prophets speak the word of God but also release people to hear God for themselves. In each of the fivefold ministries, the chief aim is Christ and His lordship; the creation of a people who will come to fullness in Christ and grow up in all things to be like Christ the Head of the Church (Ephesians 4:13–15).

Twin Curses

Is the word manipulative or controlling? What are the signs of this?

Manipulation and control are two curses currently choking the church. In my travels around the world, I have seen "prophecy" used to control and manipulate both churchgoers and leaders. These "prophets" use a word to make people do what they want or to get them on their side of an issue. We must discern whether a prophet has an ulterior motive or is trying to dishonestly gain something. We should never be indebted to someone's ministry instead of Jesus Christ.

The word *control* has two meanings — one positive and one negative. On the positive side, control involves supervising, overseeing, leading, guiding, and governing. All aspects of leadership — government of the country, management of organizations, church leadership, parenting, and school administration — require creating areas of control. In these cases, the control elements are safeguards designed to benefit others who are less mature, powerless, or in need of some type of help or support.

On the negative side, control can also mean wielding power over others, abusing others, directing people against their will, dominating, ruling, repressing, curbing, engineering events and circumstances, maneuvering people, and exerting bad influence.

These two extremes are divided by only a thin line. Responsibility and accountability hold people to the right use of control. Without these twin characteristics, governments become oppressive, managers become deceitful and demanding, church leaders fall into repression and lordly behavior, parents become domineering, and schools step into a repressive regime. It is a principle of life and democracy, as well as scriptural and godly behavior, that all leadership must be accountable.

Sadly, there are many churches and ministries where the leader's word is law. Fear of man has reached epidemic proportions in some areas of the body of Christ. All ministry without accountability is ultimately wasteful. A man can have a wonderful ministry for years and yet fall into sin or error because no one is speaking into his life. The fall from grace of people in places of power and anointing is never just personal; there is corporate fallout too, where people become embittered, hurt, and disillusioned with the individual, the church, and God Himself.

With this in mind, we must examine the motivation behind anyone who speaks prophetically. Do the words the prophet speaks match the spirit behind them? Words are only a means of communicating what has been spoken into a person's spirit. There is a difference between the spirit and the content of what is being said, but both need to line up with one another.

Motive is the line that separates Holy Spirit led prophecy from the evil spirits of divination and witchcraft. Control and manipulation have their roots in the ground of witchcraft. The nature of witchcraft is to control, while the nature of a wrong spirit is to bring control and manipulation. The two work hand-in-hand. We need to be aware of any control being exercised through prophecy. Prophetic ministry is to bring release to people, not bondage. It enables people to find the will of God for their own lives; it doesn't tie them to the prophet. Galatians 5:19–21 is clear about where the evil desire to control comes from: *"Now the deeds of the flesh are evident, which are: immorality, impurity, sensuality, idolatry, sorcery, enmities, strife, jealousy, outbursts of anger, disputes, dissensions, factions, envying, drunkenness, carousing, and things like these, of which I forewarn you, just as I have forewarned you, that those who practice such things will not inherit the kingdom of God."*

Always examine the motives of the one prophesying

Manipulating people allows the enemy to spiritually dominate us. Generally, the few specific ways in which ungodly Christian leaders fall victim to this evil include the following:

- Usurping the will of others
- Pulling rank
- Prophecy and flattery
- Dire warnings
- Not allowing any outside perspective

Usurping the will of others can occur very easily in connection with prophecy. Without proper accountability, people get used to behaving like some form of oracle, although they do not have the blessing or the approval of God for that ministry. When humility goes out of our lives, it leaves a big hole into which arrogance, self-importance, egotism, and complacency seep in. If we do not actively encourage others to judge and weigh our ministries, we lose the sense of discipline and meekness that should characterize the life of a prophet. Moses was the meekest man on the earth at that time, yet he led a whole nation to freedom. Meekness is not weakness. It is actually strength under control. Without meekness we can confuse God's will with our own needs and desires.

Humility develops accountability

One of the crassest examples I have seen of this lack of meekness occurred in a church that I had never been in contact with before. One day, they called me about a prophet who had been greatly blessing them for more than four years. The man had been wonderfully accurate and timely with his prophetic ministry. They clearly respected and admired him.

Then an unfortunate incident happened. At the end of his last visit, he spoke to a businessman in the church and prophesied to him. He told him that God wanted him to give the prophet a part of the business and that if he did so he would get a prophet's reward.

The leadership, and the businessman, was in a quandary. The prophet's track record had been impeccable, but this last prophecy greatly concerned and alarmed them. Confused, the leaders called me for my perspective, hoping an external view would give me an objective frame of reference outside of the day-to-day operation of their ministry.

Nothing about this situation felt right. Even if the prophet had been correct that God wanted him to be involved in the business, he was completely out of order in going to the guy and prophesying it to him alone. This was a directional prophecy and should have been shared with the leaders of the church first. They could have prayed together and judged the word. In these cases, leadership should act as a filter between the prophet and the people.

Moreover, this was a directional prophecy from which the prophet stood to gain something — a business and an income! This was doubly dangerous and needed very sensitive handling and proper protocol. This prophet had broken all the rules for handling revelatory prophecy. He should have spoken to leadership first, he should have never spoken to the man alone, and he should have recorded the word for the benefit of others. He did none of those things. He was out of divine order and clearly wrong.

I visited the church and asked the young businessman how he felt about the prophet.

"I really respect and admire him," he said.

"That's nice," I answered, "but that won't save your business if he is a partner."

"He's really being used by God," he said.

"That's nice," I said, "but do want to give him part of your business?"

There was silence for a few moments. He was clearly anguished. "What if my business prospers with him involved?" he asked. "I believe it will prosper anyway," I said. "The point is this man should not personally profit from a prophecy that he gave."

"But what happens if this is the will of God?" he asked me.

"If it's the will of God, God will make it clear," I replied. "But right now, this man has actually subverted your will. He has come to you, used his anointing, reputation, and gifting to put you into a position of acting against your will. Your biggest fear right now is that if you don't make him a partner, you'll somehow fall out of the will of God for the rest of your life."

The man's will had been usurped. His ability to make an effective decision had been lost, leaving him confused and agitated. Together, the businessman, the leadership, and I decided it was best to cut him off from the prophet. We suggested that he have nothing to do with him for a full year so the situation could have enough time to settle down.

Real anointing cares about the will of another

Even if the prophet's word was right, he acted wrongly. The word had to be renounced for the man's sake. This subtle manipulation of his will had to be broken. He had to be set free to pursue his business involvements without regret or fear. Had the prophet spoken the word to the leaders privately, they could have shared the burden and prayed effectively into the situation.

In this case, we cut the businessman off from any influence that would affect his right to exercise his own free will. His business is prospering well without a partner.

When I confronted the man with his sin, he told me flatly that he was a prophet of God.

"Then obviously you will be happy to talk through this issue and do the appropriate thing," I said. His reply was that all true prophets were accountable to God alone. "Ultimately, you will be," I answered, "but as part of the church you are obliged to function in relationships of openness and honesty. What you have done is illegal. You subverted this man's will and you cannot do that. You prophesied for your own gain and you cannot do that."

The church never heard from the prophet again. We cannot use our gifting to manipulate or control people. This evil motivation renders our words null and void. Prophetic ministry is supposed to bring release, not bondage.

Pulling rank is another sign of control and manipulation. This originates in someone holding a superior attitude that will only receive input from a person of peer level. We can easily disregard the words of God from people we feel are below us. On that basis, though, Naaman the Syrian would not have been healed of leprosy. After all, he had to listen to a slave girl to be cured.

We pull rank on others when we elevate our status to a point where people cannot express themselves for fear of upsetting the "man of God." There are many leaders who will not stand to be questioned. To ask for explanations or an interpretation is tantamount to rebellion in their eyes. Some leaders deliberately cultivate a separation, a distancing between them and the people.

We must beware of **prophecy and flattery**, another sure sign of the subtle manipulative process. A variety of soul ties can exist between people, not all of which are good, honorable, or profitable. A soul tie can exist between parents and children, husband and wife, best friends, disciple and mentor, and other relationships. David and Jonathan had a good soul tie, as did Paul and Timothy. We are encouraged to allow God to knit our hearts together and our lives to be fitted and framed as one (Ephesians 4:16).

I have a number of people whom I am personally discipling in areas of character, lifestyle, ministry, and leadership. There is a tie between our lives that is right and proper. It is a spiritual tie and, because friendship is emotional, also an emotional link. It is a soul tie as God is fitting us together. He is taking two threads and weaving our hearts together. We are intertwined.

A soul tie is good when there is a flow of love, affection, blessing, encouragement, and a sharpening of each other's life and gifts. We want each other to succeed and grow in God in order to fulfill His purposes. There is honor, dignity, and a desire for both to speak well of each other and want the best.

If I try to use a relationship to usurp another's will, tell him what to think, order him around, or dominate his personality, the soul tie has turned negative. I have moved a person into a place of bondage. We have all seen these domineering, one-direction relationships: overbearing husbands, strident wives, unhealthy friendships, domineering parents, and manipulative relationships in the church.

When one person continually tells another what to think or how to behave, a bad soul tie exists. More evidence of a bad soul tie can be seen when an individual is afraid to take any initiative for fear of disapproval. When a person captures another's heart by illicit means, the soul tie has become warped. These ties need to be severed and deliverance promoted. The people must be set free to be themselves before that soul tie can be reestablished properly.

Nowhere is this area more prevalent than in the relationships between men and women. There is a dynamic about close proximity between the sexes that can produce illicit relationship all too easily. Bosses and secretaries are an obvious area, pastors and administration staff another; the prophet and people can also become a disturbing relationship.

Many years ago, I was on a conference prophetic team with several people. I had just finished ministering to a person when I saw one of the other prophets praying for a very attractive woman. He was stroking her arm, and I could hear him saying, "You are an extremely attractive woman and God is going to use your beauty to do great things." When he finished, they embraced.

I couldn't believe what I was seeing. After the meeting, I went to the team and told them how uncomfortable that sort of ministry made me. The prophet had picked up on her unhappiness. She was married to a workaholic who was flying all over the world on business. She felt neglected by her husband, and the minister was feeding that.

Unfortunately, I was the junior prophet on that particular team, and the matter was quietly dismissed. Four months later, the woman left her husband and the prophet left his wife. They committed adultery and ended up together. What was supposed to be spiritual had turned carnal because an unhealthy soul tie had formed.

In prophecy, we need to be sensitive to people and the Holy Spirit. We must have our hearts on the same wavelength as the Lord's. It is very easy, in the context of the prophetic, to tune into people's weaknesses and vulnerabilities. I have seen many occasions where men have simply tuned into a woman's loneliness or pain. With a few choice words, we are all capable of detecting pain and sadness. If we are not careful, people will jump forward to receive much more than prophecy.

Sensitive to the Holy Spirit and to people

A special relationship may come into existence between the woman and the prophet. This tie can be exploited by the enemy. This is why it is so important, particularly for men, to be accountable for our sexuality. This will help us avoid carnal relationships and the kind of emotional activity that attracts and entices people. Private, one-to-one ministry must be prohibited, as the sexual dynamic can become too strong in some cases. It provides an opportunity for the enemy and that is reason enough to abandon the practice.

The reverse side of that situation is also true. There are women who actively pursue prophetic ministries for emotional, romantic, and sexual reasons. My staff could tell some stories here about how they watch over me at public events specifically.

Some women are professional victims who use their vulnerability and emotional state to disarm ministries. There is a charm, a certain learned helplessness, a carefully cultivated persona that creates scenarios where they need to be rescued.

We have to be aware of our ruling passions. Sometimes, wanting to be liked is a desire that rules us. We end up saying nice things because we think that is what people want to hear. We worry more about their reaction than if the Spirit of God is behind our prophecy. Always wanting to be liked can lead us into flattering people.

Giving **dire warnings** is another subtle form of controlling people. An element of threat is often used to gain control of people. For example, if you don't do what the prophet says, you may suffer terrible consequences. You may lose your job, your family may be hurt, or your leadership may be called into question. There is an implied threat that the blessing of God may be removed because we have not listened to the voice of the prophet.

Beware of your own ruling passions

The other, more extreme and overt threat is that of giving people over to Satan to teach them an appropriate lesson. The apostle Paul did not do this because someone did not appreciate his prophetic gift; it occurred because a man was persistently blaspheming, was resisting counsel, and needed to be dealt with on a different level. A threat, implied or otherwise, is designed to elevate the ministry to an inviolable place where it cannot be opposed.

This often goes hand-in-hand with another spiritual abuse within prophetic ministry: **not allowing any outside perspective**. It can be very unhealthy for people to be locked into one person's viewpoint and have no access to the perspective of others. In the early church, we can deduce that this was never intended to happen. With their apostolic teams and missionary journeys, key people often stayed in a location for a prolonged period of time. This type of abuse seldom occurred.

In today's environment of advanced communications and ease of travel, it should be even less of a problem. In all aspects of church life, we often need access to external dialogue. Every church should seek to be less exclusive and more open to outside comment that is reliable and trustworthy.

Prophecy is never a matter of personal interpretation. We must actively encourage people to invest in the opinions of others. Collectively, our leaders should be talking things through with people who have an objective opinion. Outsiders rarely have axes to grind or flags to wave. This is particularly helpful when prophecy has come to the corporate body of believers, giving direction and enhancement of vision.

Before a church embarks on wholesale changes in response to prophecy, it is wise to run a check by other mature ministries or prophets. When we forbid outside input, we have to rely on our own internal resources, which may not be strong or wise enough to handle the situation. Exclusiveness is a great aid to deception. Openness, honesty, and humility are great aids to the truth. Some leaders resist outside perspective for fear it will undermine their status and authority. If they are that insecure, they are probably right!

The use of the phrase, "the Lord told me," can be very unfortunate. In many cases, it is said by well-meaning people who sincerely believe that it is the right way to phrase the prophetic. In sharing a truth generally, a lot of people will say, "The Lord showed me this." If we happen to disagree with the person, it can be somewhat embarrassing for him or her to hear the words, "Actually, what you have just said is not scriptural."

Most people have no ulterior motive in using this phrase. To the pure, all things are pure. Nevertheless, it does give the enemy an opportunity to manipulate something to our detriment. Mostly, the use of the phrase highlights a degree of immaturity or insecurity. We are not always confident about revelation and how to handle it. We sometimes want other people to look up to us a little, so we use the phrase to give a boost to what we are saying. Do not make yourself an oracle.

The enemy is very good at manipulating words. If we use this phrase when we are sharing a general truth, the people we are talking with may not have the confidence or the relationship to come back on something they disagree with. We can then assume that the revelation we have shared is accurate and that we have heard correctly. In this way, a kink of deception occurs that can be strengthened and developed over time. Deception does not occur overnight; it comes in small doses over a long period of time.

Revelation requires accurate feedback

Revelation requires accurate, sensitive, and godly feedback. People must be lovingly corrected, and an environment must be created in which good feedback can occur. Where feedback is irregular or absent, pride can enter in, causing people to become resistant to authority.

With a prophetic word, feedback is absolutely essential. The content, heart attitude, method of delivery, and results achieved must all receive comment at every opportunity. What people have to say (the content) can be completely spoiled by how they say it (the delivery), mainly because their attitude was not right. People need to be instructed in what they did right and what they did wrong. Feedback is a vital part of the learning process, which, if neglected, will only store up trouble for later. The lack of proper feedback allows the enemy to put his hands on people's ministry and create disorder.

Young Christians and people being freshly inspired by revelation or the moving of the Holy Spirit are a particular target for enemy attack. We cannot allow him any room to operate. The use of the phrase, "The Lord told me," should be discouraged until people are mature enough to handle it properly and effectively.

Instead, prophetic ministries should operate in a style that is less open to manipulation and control. To avoid confusion and any appearance of manipulation, it is best to modify our language. I believe it is more rewarding to use the humble phraseology, "I believe the Lord is saying" or "I think God wants you to know."

It is absolutely vital to identify the motivation behind the prophecy. In other words, "What is the spirit of the prophet?" Often the use of a phrase like "The Lord told me," can be another sign that the individual may be trying to engineer something that is not of God. It means that the only way forward into clarification and understanding may be through confrontation. When someone declares, "God has shown me," it gives the listener very few options. It robs people of the initiative to respond with a question if one is necessary.

People of little confidence will feel that they cannot possibly respond to the prophecy. It can be used quite ruthlessly by some people. It can be a complete departure from the gospel of grace and kindness. The gospel is redemptive, and prophecy is intended to liberate people into a wider expression of God's love. Most people preface their prophecies with that phrase because they have very little confidence in the prophecy itself. They are trying to invest the message with an authority and gravitas they themselves do not possess. They are also trying to make it difficult for people to counteract their words. They are seeking to endow their own lives and ministries with an authority that the Lord has not given them. As well as being incredibly arrogant and ill-mannered, the constant use of this phrase may reveal an inadequacy that is quite desperate.

Where there is no grace there is control

Revelation has a power all its own. In general, it does not need to be prefaced with "The Lord showed me." Our spirit will always recognize truth. The Holy Spirit, the Spirit of truth, has His own way of impacting our spirits. He does not need help from a prophet in that regard.

I am always amazed at people who use this form of expression. In many cases, the needs of their own lives seem blindingly obvious. If they are hearing God tell them things, how is it they have never heard some basic truths for themselves? Why didn't God tell that man to love his wife, or father his children properly? Why didn't the woman hear God say that worry, anxiety, and bitterness should be exchanged for trust, faith, and forgiveness? Why didn't those people hear God talk to them about giving financially, being faithful and committed, standing with leaders, giving the gospel to the lost, and about the Holy Spirit's work among the poor?

People are selective about truth. We take on board things that will bless us and push away those truths that will disrupt our normal routines. If we are not prepared to hear the Lord speak the whole truth and order our lives on a regular basis, we should not dishonor Him by prefacing things we do hear with, "The Lord says."

It is this kind of "hyper-spirituality" that is anathema to God's Spirit and can be a major factor in control and manipulation. Where there is no grace, there is control. Where there is no love, there is an outlook that sees people as objects to be moved around according to our own purposes. We maneuver people into places where they will have the most use for us, just like we place our home or office furniture.

It is a major crime against the body of Christ when we fail to see the value of all people, to look upon them as God sees them, to see the best in people, and to bring the life of Jesus to the surface.

A "hyper-spiritual" attitude motivated to preserve its own life seeks to make everything deeply spiritual and mystical. It cannot bear the thought of others knowing what it knows. It seeks to make the gifts and knowledge of

God inaccessible to people. The very thought of equipping and activating the saints so that they can do the work of the ministry is an abomination to such people. The root of this disease is found in control and manipulation, and in a desire to dominate others spiritually so that they become dependent upon our ministries. People with such an attitude need serious help to realize the love of God in a deeper way. They may require deliverance from inadequacy, insecurity, and a dominating lifestyle.

> *God is redemptive, not ruthless*

Prophecy seeks to release people into the fullness of God's desires and purposes for them. Prophecy will always cooperate with, and be founded on, the glory of revealed truth. It is an awesome thing to sit before the Lord with an open Bible and have the Holy Spirit speak through the pages, bringing confidence, joy, real change, and renewal. It is a delight to sit in a teaching meeting where there is anointed exposition of Scripture. Look around in those meetings and see the concentration and the joy of learning on the faces of the listeners.

Revelation releases joy. The entrance of personal revelation has always left me wanting to adore Jesus, to kick off my shoes and dance, to shout with joy, and to beam with pleasure at God.

Prophecy and Paradox

> *Prophecy works into the paradox of life in that it should clearly state what we are doing well whilst graciously challenging where we need to change.*

We all live in paradox. A paradox is two apparently contrasting ideas in the same issue. We learn to look at both/and, not merely either/or to discover the truth.

For example, someone could rightly point out that the church is a building (1 Peter 2:4–5). Another would be equally as correct in determining that the church is a body (Ephesians 1:22–23, 4:15–16). Both are right. A paradox is concerned with extremes or opposites and how we live with both. A building is rigid, inflexible, and unchanging. A body is fluid, flexible, and always adjusting. The key to knowing which to apply is concerned with primacy and the objective of the Holy Spirit.

If we are in a situation where the Father is building relationships throughout the church, then clearly we must use the church as a house and household of faith. Church as a building is concerned with the dynamics of being, who we are becoming, and establishing good relationships. Love is rigid, inflexible, and unchanging, which is a great way to describe a constant. God's nature is constant, in that He is steadfast, unchanging, faithful, and totally committed to grace and patience with truth.

If we are looking at developing the giftings, anointing, and ministries of people then we are occupied with church as a body. We become involved with vision, training, equipping, releasing, and empowering of people. We are concerned with what they do more than perhaps who they are becoming. This aspect of church is mostly concerned about doing, functionality, and ministry.

The circumstances dictate which part of the paradox we get to move in with the Holy Spirit. We all live in paradox and we must seek to understand life and people in that context.

Often we can try to make someone out to be all bad. We either demonize people or ascribe something angelic to them. Both are false. People are usually a mixture. It is not wrong; it is life and therefore subject to change.

God's heart is constant as we learn to grow and change. He bears with our weaknesses and inadequacies because He knows what He is making us into regarding sonship and maturity. Most people have some redeeming qualities even if they are buried very well inside a personality that sets our teeth on edge.

The Lord always speaks to our potential as well as our actual development. He is present–future in His heart towards us. He loves to stand in the gap between our present and future, like any good intercessor, and pray for us (Romans 8:34; Hebrews 7:25). When prophecy arises out of a heart soaked in prayer it has the virtue of seeing people from God's perspective. We see who they are now, including possible, current struggles and mindsets. We also see who they are becoming and the purposes of God in present circumstances. Good prophecy marries both together so that we are opened up to all the great possibilities of God and wisely challenged about existing issues. The Lord loves us to see who we are becoming.

God speaks to our potential as well as the actual

The key to paradox in people and prophecy is sensitivity, both to the Holy Spirit and to humanity. Sensitivity means that we only do what the Father is doing and we only say what He is saying! Avoid your own opinions. Try to be pure in the process of how you think and perceive. Especially, if you are emotionally invested in the situation, you must exert real transparency, honesty, and care.

How do we handle negative prophecy? The gift of discerning of spirits enables us to determine the spiritual origin or source of actual events and spoken words. There can be an immediate "witness" in our spirits to something that is said or done. This must be confirmed in other ways too, by Scripture and by agreement with people of maturity.

Where there is no inner witness to prophecy, we must exercise our hearts more cautiously. In this careful consideration, we attempt to discover the following:

- Is the source of the word an evil spirit?
- Is the word originating in the prophet's human spirit? Is it the spirit of man?

With words of judgment, we must understand that true prophecy does not produce slaves. Words that are negative, judgmental, and condemning can create a wrong form of fear.

There is a fear of God that is right and healthy; I love God, but I'm afraid of Him as well. It's a paradox — the early church walked in the fear of the Lord and the comfort of the Holy Spirit. We can be so afraid of God that only the Holy Spirit can comfort us, but this type of prophecy will not produce that.

Prophecy can speak directly or indirectly into situations

A prophecy must be good news, even if that news is "repent," and words that highlight sin must contain a clear call to repentance. This type of word is called contending prophecy. It highlights issues that must be addressed. It can be used directly or indirectly. Nathan on one occasion used the indirect approach to speak to King David.

> *Then the LORD sent Nathan to David. And he came to him and said, "There were two men in one city, the one rich and the other poor. The rich man had a great many flocks and herds. But the poor man had nothing except one little ewe lamb which he bought and nourished; and it grew up together with him and his children. It would eat of his bread and drink of his cup and lie in his bosom, and was like a daughter to him.*
>
> *"Now a traveler came to the rich man, and he was unwilling to take from his own flock or his own herd, to prepare for the wayfarer who had come to him; rather he took the poor man's ewe lamb and prepared it for the man who had come to him."*
>
> *Then David's anger burned greatly against the man, and he said to Nathan, "As the LORD lives, surely the man who has done this deserves to die. He must make restitution for the lamb fourfold, because he did this thing and had no compassion."*
>
> *Nathan then said to David, "You are the man! Thus says the LORD God of Israel, 'It is I who anointed you king over Israel and it is I who delivered you from the hand of Saul. I also gave you your master's house and your master's wives into your care, and I gave you the house of Israel and Judah; and if that had been too little, I would have added to you many more things like these!*
>
> *'Why have you despised the word of the LORD by doing evil in His sight? You have struck down Uriah the Hittite with the sword, have taken his wife to be your wife, and have killed him with the sword of the sons of Ammon. Now therefore, the sword shall never depart from your house, because you have despised Me and have taken the wife of Uriah the Hittite to be your wife.'*

"Thus says the LORD, 'Behold, I will raise up evil against you from your own household; I will even take your wives before your eyes and give them to your companion, and he will lie with your wives in broad daylight. Indeed you did it secretly, but I will do this thing before all Israel, and under the sun.'"

Then David said to Nathan, "I have sinned against the LORD." And Nathan said to David, "The LORD also has taken away your sin; you shall not die. However, because by this deed you have given occasion to the enemies of the LORD to blaspheme, the child also that is born to you shall surely die." So Nathan went to his house (2 Samuel 12:1–15).

Nathan told a story to David who responded very forthrightly at what he perceived to be an injustice. Nathan was able to get into David's heart and bring resolution to a moral problem in the life of the king.

A more direct approach is seen in the book of Revelation, in the letters to the church in Asia. In the message to the church at Ephesus we read:

To the angel of the church in Ephesus write:

The One who holds the seven stars in His right hand, the One who walks among the seven golden lampstands, says this: "I know your deeds and your toil and perseverance, and that you cannot tolerate evil men, and you put to the test those who call themselves apostles, and they are not, and you found them to be false; and you have perseverance and have endured for My name's sake, and have not grown weary.

"But I have this against you, that you have left your first love. Therefore remember from where you have fallen, and repent and do the deeds you did at first; or else I am coming to you and will remove your lampstand out of its place — unless you repent. Yet this you do have, that you hate the deeds of the Nicolaitans, which I also hate. He who has an ear, let him hear what the Spirit says to the churches. To him who overcomes, I will grant to eat of the tree of life which is in the Paradise of God" (Revelation 2:1–7).

This type of prophecy contends for a better way. Where standards have dropped, then mediocrity must be addressed so that excellence may be reestablished.

Ephesus was a good hardworking church. They had stamina, strength, and were wise enough not to be taken in by deceitful men. Yet they had left their first love. They had stepped back from a place of intimacy and had not continued to grow in worship as a lifestyle. In the evangelical tradition we have made the same error. We have elevated the Great Commission above the First Commandment.

We must know what we are contending *for*, not just what we are fighting *against*. Contending prophecy must have a grace base, otherwise it becomes negative prophecy. Ephesus was a good church and in many respects to be applauded. The discrepancy they are experiencing would have eventually stripped them of the presence of God if left unchecked.

A wholesome and positive way exists to deal with negative prophecy; it can achieve the purposes of God if done correctly. Revelation 2–3, for example, contains several prophetic words to the churches in Asia. They were not all complimentary! We need to note the context, the words, and the response required from each church.

In Revelation 2:2, the prophetic word to the church in Ephesus is recorded: "*I know your deeds and your toil and perseverance, and that you cannot tolerate evil men, and you put to the test those who call themselves apostles, and they are not, and you found them to be false.*" I believe we're going to see this happen a lot more in the next ten years in the church. A lot of people who have given themselves the title of apostle will be tested in the season that is coming. I think there are more false apostles than real ones out there right now. I don't mean demonic apostles, but ministries that are ignorant about what an apostle really is. Persuading a number of churches that they need your ministry doesn't make you an apostle. No person can confer a title like that; it's something God brings you into. Pastor, prophet, evangelist, teacher, apostle: these are job descriptions, not titles.

Jesus taught us to reject every title except for these three: servant, steward, and slave. We are all servants of the Lord. When we mature into the place of being an excellent servant, God promotes us into stewardship. Stewards care for others and carry a burden for the people around them. When we become excellent stewards, we are again promoted. The bond slave is the highest spiritual designation in the kingdom of heaven. The apostles in Scripture — Paul, Peter, John, James, and the rest — all used the same approach. Being an apostle was just something they did, a word that described their actions. Their real identities were as bond slaves of Christ.

In each opening greeting their letters to the churches of these men — Paul, James, Peter, John and Jude — all used the title bond slave. Paul used it on three occasions when communicating to the churches at Rome, Philippi, and in a personal letter to Titus. Even the demonic realm recognizes these titles and their importance.

> *It happened that as we were going to the place of prayer, a slave girl having a spirit of divination met us, who was bringing her masters much profit by fortune-telling. Following after Paul and us, she kept crying out, saying, "These men are bondservants of the Most High God, who are proclaiming to you the way of salvation." She continued doing this for*

many days. But Paul was greatly annoyed, and turned and said to the spirit, "I command you in the name of Jesus Christ to come out of her!" And it came out at that very moment. (Acts 16:16–18)

The spirit of divination in the woman did not call Paul and Silas apostles. It referred to them as "bond slaves of the Most High God". Why is it that the demonic realm can recognize something that the church cannot see?

Jesus himself spoke openly and passionately about this issue. We read these words in Matthew 23:8–12: *"But do not be called Rabbi; for One is your Teacher, and you are all brothers. Do not call anyone on earth your father; for One is your Father, He who is in heaven. Do not be called leaders; for One is your Leader, that is, Christ. But the greatest among you shall be your servant. Whoever exalts himself shall be humbled; and whoever humbles himself shall be exalted."*

Do not allow yourself to be called Rabbi, father, or leader. Titles are for God. Call yourself a servant, as Christ did. The apostles were firmly in that tradition of understanding the spiritual designations of servant, steward, and bond slave.

Ministry titles are: servant, steward and bond slave.

The Revelation 2 prophecy to the Ephesian church continued: "*You have perseverance and have endured for My name's sake, and have not grown weary. But I have this against you, that you have left your first love. Therefore remember from where you have fallen, and repent and do the deeds you did at first; or else I am coming to you and will remove your lampstand out of its place — unless you repent*" (vv. 3–5). This was a hardworking church that had come to a place where its function and operation actually took them away from fulfilling God's commandment to love Him first. Churches are often in danger of ignoring the Great Commandment in order to fulfill the Great Commission. But loving God with all of our heart, soul, mind, and strength, and loving our neighbor as we love ourselves must take precedence.

Anybody who has been in ministry knows how easy it is to wind up in an excellent working relationship with Jesus, but a lousy friendship. All of our relating to Him can become based on our call or ministry. We pray about every aspect of our work — youth, children, finances, pastoring, cells, vision, missions — and forget to leave time to worship, thank, bless, or wait on Him. Most leaders don't know how to meditate on God and then wonder why they don't have any access to deep truth in their personal lives. We have to set aside time to be with God. That is what this prophetic word was all about.

The secret of longevity in the anointing is to spend most of it on your relationship with God. Take the anointing that is readily available for worship, praise, rejoicing, and thanksgiving. Move in these anointings to create a powerful inner life of intimacy with the Lord.

80% of the anointing is for the sake of intimacy

Take the anointing that is on all of the fruit of the Spirit and allow your inner man to abide in a greater state of being before the Lord. Practice these continuously and you will never have a problem finding and experiencing the manifest presence of God.

We must have an idea of the situation and circumstances in order to bring an effective word of correction that will achieve God's purposes. Negative prophecy must be rooted in the context of what is happening. We must give commendations to people in areas where they are doing well or bearing up in a godly fashion under intolerable strain.

We can then highlight the area that God wants to touch and that will require change, giving a clear call to repentance. In the prophecy to the church of Ephesus, a negative is spoken in order to achieve a positive. It follows this pattern:

- Understand the context of what the church is facing. (v. 2)
- Express areas where commendations are relevant. (vv. 3, 6)
- Highlight the area requiring change. (v. 4)
- Give a clear call to repentance. (v. 5)

God knew the Ephesians' deeds, toils, and perseverance. He knew how good they were at discerning false teaching and motives, and how they never tired in their efforts for Him. But He also had to deal with a sin issue. When the Holy Spirit comes along, He puts His finger right on the sin and names it. The enemy operates in vagueness: he whispers that there is sin in the camp but never gives any specifics. However, the Holy Spirit is always specific and accurate, and when He names a sin, He is prepared to deal with it. When the Holy Spirit is on our case, He exposes God's grace and mercy at the same time.

We can see this protocol again in the prophetic word to the church at Pergamum in Revelation 2:13–17:

> *I know where you dwell, where Satan's throne is; and you hold fast My name, and did not deny My faith even in the days of Antipas, My witness, My faithful one, who was killed among you, where Satan dwells. But I have a few things against you, because you have there some who hold the teaching of Balaam, who kept teaching Balak to put a stumbling block before the sons of Israel, to eat things sacrificed to idols and to commit acts of immorality. So you also have some who in the same way hold the teaching of the Nicolaitans.*
>
> *Therefore repent; or else I am coming to you quickly, and I will make war against them with the sword of My mouth. He who has an ear, let him hear what the Spirit says to the churches.*

Heaven was effusive in its praise for this church. They had moved into the most occult part of town and survived the martyrdom of one of their own. They lived and worked right where Satan's throne was. God loved their willingness to dare on His behalf.

But He also had to highlight a significant sin issue: involvement in evil doctrine. The church at Pergamum were compromising on truth. They were under constant pressure not to be outspoken. The enemy always wants the gospel watered down, diluted of its power.

Tolerance is the contemporary spirit of this present age. The church is being pushed into secular humanism and political correctness at every turn. A war will break out on this line regarding tolerance, and we must be prepared to pay the price if we truly believe that we serve the one true God. Contending prophecy enables us to both bless and prepare people to better endure and overcome the present conflict around their life and ministry.

Tolerance is the spirit of this age

In the middle of this occult territory, this church had to live in the tension of a clash between two kingdoms. Unless we have an internal place to rest and connect with the Holy Spirit, we will be pushed back by the enemy. The only thing that makes us stand is who we are on the inside and who we know God wants to be for us. When we learn how to live with God as our refuge and strong tower, the enemy cannot stop us. The church in Pergamum had lost its ability to live in the spirit and was being blown by the wind of evil around it.

When I used to do missions work in Asia, I would often visit Christians living in Islamic strongholds. I could easily identify the Christian leaders who put the necessary time into their personal relationship with God — they lived in a place of peace above the spiritual war raging around them. The people who had not invested in their relationship with God were being crushed by the weight of the opposition around them.

If God has put you in a war zone, the one thing you need to do is spend more time with God than you do with people. The people who succeeded in those Muslim countries often spent eight or nine hours a day with God. They could accomplish more in two hours than most people could all day. They would have breakthrough words of knowledge and healing. When they came out of the presence of God, they were fully charged. Nothing fazed them. They carried a favor to do something and they had an ability to change things.

Contending prophecy turns us back to the purposes of God. In the worst part of town, that church had been living under the crushing pressure of the enemy. They had started giving some ground in order to have peace. They allowed some people to hold different doctrines and share them with others. But God wanted them to be pure in word and deed, and His call was for them to repent.

If we do not contend for one another we will fight against each other

Contending prophetic words produce repentance, not condemnation. Words that contain no positive way forward and leave people feeling totally condemned should be resisted, or we may allow the enemy to get a foothold in the church. This kind of negative input is ungodly and unscriptural and needs to be dealt with. One of the hallmarks of enemy activity is an accusing spirit.

Accusation is his life work and trademark. He constantly accuses the brethren. Every demon has a weapon of accusation in their hands. Therefore, we can identify the spirit that is attacking us by what we are actually being accused of. If we are wrongly accused of domination and control, it is probably a spirit of domination and control accusing us. In this manner, we can chase down every accusation and bring it into the light of truth.

A friend of mine, a minister, was accused by the media of being a pedophile. The man was totally innocent, but his name was slandered throughout the region. Desperate for help, he called me for advice.

"There are two things at work here," I said. "One is an accusing spirit, and you have to take authority over that. But you also have to take authority over the spirit of pedophilia in the whole area." The enemy had tipped its hand about what was going on in the region. I knew that if the church took authority over both the accusation and the spirit of pedophilia, something would break for the positive. The enemy's accusation was vital intelligence about the war he was waging in the area. God had allowed this accusation to come so that the church would know what to pray.

Accusing spirits always reveal their own handiwork

The region's churches responded by gathering to pray against the spirit of accusation and pedophilia. After two weeks of solid prayer, a breakthrough happened. A whole pedophilia ring was exposed in the area. Many were arrested. It was almost like God goaded the enemy to attack someone who was pure so that He could reveal what was really at work.

We need to be aware of spiritual things. We should understand what the process of the enemy is and what God's plan is to deal with it. We can attack the evil spirit that is attacking us because God has given us permission to defeat it. God allows in His wisdom what He could easily prevent by His power. The purpose of the demonic is to teach you how to rest in the power of the Holy Spirit.

The enemy always seeks to intimidate us. He wants to paralyze us into inactivity. A lot of these things come through words that appear prophetic, but are anything but. The enemy loves to cloak himself in spiritual terms, capitalizing on the fact that the prophetic is not rational or logical, it is spiritual. This mystery provides good cover for him, so we need to be impeccably clean and pure in who we are in Christ.

Lulling Christians into a state of passivity is the enemy's great strategy. He tries to penetrate the church, demoralize the leadership and key people, and subvert the body into accepting a more passive way of living. He doesn't want us to be active in our faith, or be bold or confident about anything.

Not every incorrect word is the result of an enemy spirit however; sometimes, it is the spirit of man at work. The spirit of man wants to manipulate and control people, usually for power, monetary, or sexual gain. Prophecy is then used to make people do what the individual wants.

> *Passivity is always destructive*

We need to be especially aware of people who "prophesy" their own opinions. They give a negative word that may contain trace elements of truth but is really a platform for what they think. They tag a "you need to repent" message on the end to give it some kind of credence. There may well be some areas that do require attention, and it is always good to let the light of God shine, no matter who seems to be holding the flashlight! Never dismiss truth because you don't like the truth giver. Our allegiance must always be to the truth.

People add the repentance message in order to feel spiritual and safe. Any opposite response to their word can be called rebellion and disobedience, pride or arrogance. Some situations simply do not deserve the weight of that kind of prophecy, and people will rightly reject that type of word.

Many people cannot differentiate between their own opinions and the word of the Lord; they cannot tell the difference between a righteous anger and the gall and bitterness of their own frustration. These people need help and support to enable them to mature. Again, the place of feedback is vital as we can not let people get away with things in prophecy. If we do, we are storing up trouble for the church.

If we have a contending word to bring, there is a procedure to follow that will glorify God.

1. We must get our own attitudes right by getting rid of the plank in our own eye before sharing the word with responsible people. A contending word must first contend with our flesh, our attitudes, and our own negative motivations.

2. Fasting and praying is a wonderful way to purify our motives and enable the Holy Spirit to filter out our opinions, frustrations, and resentments. Try holding on to frustration while your stomach is growling!

3. During that time before the Lord, we need to become obedient ourselves. We must ensure that we have nothing against anyone. Put things right if there is a problem area.

4. Share the word with leaders and mature people and allow them to judge it before it is delivered publicly.

A peculiar responsibility exists in contending prophecy, and we must carry it out with integrity. In many instances, He gives us a contending word as part of the process of bringing change into our own lives. If we find it easy to give these types of words, then something is wrong with us and, in all likelihood, we may require ministry ourselves. Be careful with prophecy that contends because truth always rebounds!

I would not allow people to give contending words in the first few years of their development in the prophetic gifting. We must earn the right to bring that type of word. We do that by our character, our service, and by demonstrating our love for God and His church. It is good to keep people on a diet of edification, exhortation, and comforting words until they really know the tenderness of God's heart toward His people. I would encourage such people to filter contending words through mature people who may well give that prophecy themselves if it is proved out. Of course, we can always credit the source.

Allowing a person to deliver a contending word should mark a change in their ministries and in their maturity. It is evidence to all that this person is "growing up" in the gift and can be trusted by their local leaders.

There is a cost in giving contending prophecy. It should not be easy. Pain is involved and heart-searching is necessary. Being right before the Lord is a prerequisite.

Track Record

All these tests are designed to enable us to process what the Lord is actually saying to us. We learn to filter out unhelpful voices and bad practice. We are also developing the track record of the people in our midst who are seeking to grow in the prophetic gift. Everyone who prophesies must value their credibility highly. Building a good track record is the very least that we can do if we want to be excellent in how we represent the Lord.

When our words are tested and evaluated we should have the attitude of wanting to grow in the Spirit, above all else. Accountability is about loving the learning inherent in each set of circumstances. Approach people with a hunger to learn, grow and become. No matter how clumsy people will treat us, get past that to the learning that is available. All my best disciples have had that character trait in abundance!

I can appreciate that at times it may be difficult to apply this to the person prophesying. It may be someone who is just starting to move out in prophecy on a regular basis or, alternatively, someone from outside the church with whom we are not familiar. However, in the latter case we must try to get a recommendation for his ministry from a reputable source if we can.

Asking for recommendations from others is an important and worthwhile thing to do. Leaders must always be protective of their flocks. However, please bear in mind that this is not just the track record of the prophet that we should worry about. We need to examine the track records of all ministries: the teacher, the evangelist, the itinerant preacher, the worship leader, the deliverance ministry, the healing ministry. Anyone who has a public ministry needs to have a track record that is observable.

It is important to note with new people that we must be gracious and allow for their learning experience. Good quality and loving feedback is absolutely vital. Don't let them get away with anything, not even the smallest mistake. Do put every correction in the context of love, kindness, approval, and a desire to see them grow and develop. This is called fathering. We must look to develop people in the prophetic gift and into the prophetic ministry. Please note that the two are quite different! In terms of gifting, everyone has prophetic potential that needs developmental and training. However, we need more than potential to develop the gift into a ministry; we need hard evidence. We need proof positive that their words are coming to pass and that God is with them in a ministry capacity.

Accountability is about cultivating the passions of freedom

In Deuteronomy 18:22 we read, *"If the thing does not come about or come true, that is the thing which the LORD has not spoken The prophet has spoken it presumptuously."*

People must have a track record of their words being fulfilled. If there is no confirmation after judging the word, or no fulfillment of the prophecy, we must go back to the person who gave the word.

Other people who may know us may witness to the word, yet that is not necessarily confirmation. A witness is a good indicator that will inspire us to press on in judging the word correctly.

False Versus Poor Prophecy

False prophecy, at its heart, is deceptive. It involves a subtle and often deliberate attempt to lead people away from the Lord. It may well raise up men and women in place of God. It will move people away from the vital place of humility before God that all of us should enjoy. Humility of heart is a major characteristic of any public ministry in the body of Christ. Some people confuse boldness with arrogance or meekness with weakness.

Boldness comes from a confidence in God that arises out of our intimate knowledge of who He is and our inheritance in Christ. Meekness is simply strength under control. Humility and confidence go together for they are both sides of the same coin. Sadly, we seldom see them paired together in people.

A humble heart is one that is dedicated to the truth, however costly. It seeks out the truth like a lover. False prophecy creates idols, often by putting something or someone in between the people and God. Anything in prophecy that pushes God a step from His people must be disregarded.

Poor prophecy, on the other hand, needs to be understood. Prophecy can be impure because it mixes our own thoughts and opinions so that the word can become distorted. People can put some padding around the word that devalues the prophecy. A lot of this can be attributed to style and upbringing. If we live among people who are long-winded in prophecy, we may well take on that characteristic. If that is the case, we may not know how to handle a short word from God. Some of the most profound words I have spoken have been one-sentence prophecies.

Sometimes prophecy can be poor because we have borrowed a style and a language from someone else. In some Pentecostal circles, I am not regarded as prophetic because my style is so different. I do not clamp my hand on people's heads, roaring some prophetic words in an archaic language with spittle flying everywhere. I use the same language and tone of voice in prophecy that I do over a quiet dinner. Be yourself. We are normal people in touch with a supernatural God. When we really touch God's heart completely, we discover that He is the most normal, sane, well-balanced person in the universe — except when He isn't! God is normal, except when He is being extraordinary. We misunderstand God so much, a fact particularly seen in how we handle the prophetic.

Discipleship puts a face on maturity

Some people have to dress up their prophecies by using fancy language or raising their volume or speaking for a certain length of time. This is not evidence of the Holy Spirit.

Weak prophecy can also occur. This happens when we move out on a feeling or just a couple of words. There is a school of thought that says, "If all you have are a couple of words, then you must step out in faith, open your mouth, and God will fill it."

They often quote the verses of Mark 10:18–20, Luke 12:11–12, and Luke 21:12–15, which, at first glance, seem to say, "Take no thought of what you should say; I will be with your mouth." However, we take these Scriptures out of context when we use them in connection with prophecy. All these Scriptures clearly refer to situations where people are being dragged before synagogues and rulers who are demanding an explanation for the preaching of the Gospel. In those circumstances, God will give us wisdom (not prophecy) that will be difficult to resist. It is the same promise that God gave Moses before he went to Pharaoh to ask for Israel's release in Exodus 4:10–12.

Many people think it is wrong to plan or rehearse prophecy. While we cannot manufacture a word, we shouldn't kiss our brains goodbye either. The definition of a lot of prophecy in this post-charismatic era is "an empty thought passing through an empty head."

In the Old Testament, if God spoke to the prophet in Beersheba and gave him a word for the king at Jerusalem, it would have taken him several days to get there. During that journey, he probably prayed, rehearsed, and planned the delivery of the word, particularly if it was going to bother the king — after all, it could mean the prophet's death! He might have even written it out before he got there. More than a third of the Old Testament is recorded prophecy.

Spontaneous prophecy has its place. However, the Scripture has at least as much to say about planned and rehearsed prophecy. The reality is that we need both methods to be judged and weighed effectively. One is not better than the other. They are simply different.

> *We cannot be spontaneous unless we have an alternative*

Everyone has to grow up through the baby phase of moving in prophecy. When a person first begins to prophesy, we sometimes think that because our heart is pounding like a jackhammer, our palms are sweaty, our hair is standing up on our neck, we sense the presence of God, and we have a few words rattling around our head, we must step out and speak. Never assume! Very often, when I have encountered those same feelings, it has simply been God trying to get my attention. It is often His way of letting me know that He wants to say something to me personally. It does not indicate at this point that He wants me to share it with others.

Application

How do we apply the tests?

When we visit the doctor for a full medical examination, we undergo a battery of tests designed to check our fitness and health. One or two positive results do not guarantee a clean bill of health. There is a series of tests that are given to determine any major health problems. If we fail these tests, we are in trouble — we cannot proceed any further.

This is similar to testing prophecy. If the word fails any of the tests we have just laid out, we cannot take the word any further. We must go back down the line to the one who prophesied to ask some specific questions and try to get some resolution.

In the medical world, if a person gets through the initial major test series, they are subjected to another battery of different tests in order to determine the general level of fitness. Similarly, in prophecy there is a further series of observations that need to be made with regard to determining some of the finer points of the word. This second series of checks will enable us to determine what kind of word it is and the appropriate response we can make. It will also provide us with some idea of the wider issues involved in following up the word.

The word has passed the main tests and can be accepted. We now have to ask a series of questions so that we know what to do with it and can gauge its relevance for the present or coming season. The subsequent areas of consideration and therefore concern are:

- Focus on outcomes. Is an outcome far away in the future or close at hand? Are there any preparations we must make as we cooperate with the Holy Spirit?
- Recognize that all prophecy is partial. What part is the word actually speaking into?

- What type of prophecy is it? Is it a now, a future, a confirming or a new word?
- Permission. Never assume that because you have the word that you have permission to give it.
- What is the process required to enable us to walk this out before the Lord?
- When should we begin to make adjustments?

Focus on Outcomes

With prophecy, our main emphasis has to be on evaluating the word prior to delivery. With words of correction and direction, the prophecy needs to be checked before it is delivered in the public arena. There is also a retrospective testing that goes on, because a prophecy may pass all the main tests and subsidiary ones, yet take years to be fulfilled. Caleb waited forty-five years before his prophecy from Moses was fulfilled and he came into his own land of Hebron (Joshua 14). David waited twenty-four years before Samuel's word about being king finally came to pass.

> *After the calling comes the training*

In 1975, I received a prophetic word about having a significant ministry in the American church. In 1991, after having prayed and believed God for seventeen years, the Holy Spirit finally gave me permission to take up some opportunities to preach in the United States. In 2002, I started living in the states for six months a year. In 2004, I moved my office and full-time base to California, twenty-nine years — and six U.S. presidents — after that first prophecy. In the time between a word and its fulfillment, we must face the issue and the battle of whether the prophecy is true and if the timing is of God.

The temptation is to feel that if the word does not happen during a specific time frame, it must not have been God speaking it. This thinking can lead people to let go of a right word.

Of course, we cannot just spend our lives waiting for a prophetic word to come to pass. We must get on with our lives and be involved in doing God's work for now, while at the same time using the prophecy to keep us in touch with God's agenda for our future. Prophecy always gives us a prayer agenda. While I continued to work in the United Kingdom and Europe, doing prophecy schools and building churches, I prayed for America. I continually asked God to speak to me about that great country.

When the Lord spoke to me about the American church, I had no outlet for those words. Because of that, I have spent many hundreds of hours in prayer, speaking those words back to God in confidence of their fulfillment. The prophecies gave me a prayer agenda for the United States. When I first began visiting America, I was delighted to see that many of the things I had been praying about for years were beginning to happen. Such things as embracing the apostolic ministry, understanding the role of Ephesians 4:11 ministries, cell group dynamics, nonreligious Christianity, evangelism by church planting, the restructuring of church government, the fire of heaven falling on key ministries and churches, the purifying work of the Holy Spirit, the return to preaching the kingdom, and the training and development of the saints are all high on the agenda of the American church. The result of all that prayer is that I feel completely at home in the United States and have been received wonderfully well wherever I have ministered.

We need to focus on outcomes as far as time will allow us. Has the prophecy produced any negative elements? What are the positive things that the Spirit is highlighting to us? In Deuteronomy 13:1–5, Moses laid out what should happen if a prophetic word takes glory away from God.

> *If a prophet or a dreamer of dreams arises among you and gives you a sign or a wonder, and the sign or the wonder comes true, concerning which he spoke to you, saying, "Let us go after other gods (whom you have not known) and let us serve them," you shall not listen to the words of that prophet or that dreamer of dreams; for the LORD your God is testing you to find out if you love the LORD your God with all your heart and with all your soul.*
>
> *You shall follow the LORD your God and fear Him; and you shall keep His commandments, listen to His voice, serve Him, and cling to Him. But that prophet or that dreamer of dreams shall be put to death, because he has counseled rebellion against the LORD your God who brought you from the land of Egypt and redeemed you from the house of slavery, to seduce you from the way in which the LORD your God commanded you to walk So you shall purge the evil from among you.*

We must learn to work with prophetic ministry — both the gift we are growing internally and the prophetic input we receive from outside the work. Internally, we need to change the way prophecy is administered. The government of the church cannot be usurped and the flock cannot be damaged. Yet at the same time, the word of the Lord must be given free rein, no matter how unpleasant the word of God is to the local leadership.

True prophecy promotes obedience at all levels of church life, from the leadership through to the youngest believer. It should bring closeness to God even if we have to turn 180 degrees through repentance. The prophet and the prophecy must exalt Jesus and promote a godly response.

Accuracy in prophecy is not enough. Miracles, signs, and wonders are not the evidence of a true prophet. If any prophetic word is accompanied by signs and wonders, we must still evaluate it by these criteria. Where does faith in this prophetic word actually take us? Does it take us away from God's purposes, away from His morality? I know people today who, ten years ago, were given a prophetic word that they would have a particular ministry and travel to certain places. At the time, nobody else really witnessed to it, but nevertheless, they held on to it and they have now become isolated from the body of Christ. They are no longer in any church. They are in isolation, on their own. The outcome of that prophecy has been profoundly negative, but they are still holding on to it.

> *Prophecy allows us to cooperate with the process, knowing that the outcome is secure in God's hand*

To the real prophet, the glory of God is absolutely essential. We live to see Him glorified, honored, and His name uplifted. The model that John the Baptist displayed (i.e., "He must increase, I must decrease") is the hallmark of a true prophetic spirit. We simply must glorify the Lord Jesus.

The primary ministry of the Holy Spirit is to reveal and glorify Jesus, and we have to guard against any revelation that emphasizes a person or a ministry more than Jesus. True prophecy always wants to reproduce the character of Jesus in people. In my conferences, I don't apologize for being strong on the necessity of character. True prophetic ministry has to be concerned with the nature, character, morality, righteousness, and holiness of the work because that is who God is. It is such an essential part of prophetic gifting. Romans 14:17 lists righteousness, peace, and joy as the main products of life in the Spirit. Ephesians 5:9 says that *"the fruit of the Light consists in all goodness and righteousness and truth."* Galatians 5:22–23 speaks about the nine forms of fruit produced by the Holy Spirit.

Where that fruit is not evident in the life of a person, we must be careful. In Matthew 7:16, we are told, "You will know them by their fruits." It is important that in any kind of ministry, especially prophetic ministry, we always insist on character before gift.

Does the prophecy arm rival factions? Is it divisive? Is it against the vision? Does it speak against leadership? There may be problems in a church, but prophecy is not the way to solve them! Using prophecy in this way will allow the enemy to gain lots of footholds in the church. It will allow our carnality to oppose the work of the Spirit.

Do we sense that the outcome — in other words, the fulfillment of the word — is still some time in the future? Then we must focus on preparing the way of the Lord. Alternatively, is the completion of the word close at hand? What changes will we need to make on both fronts if we are to realize what the Father intends?

How do we as a leadership, a prophetic individual, and as a church body make the necessary adjustments to the operation of the ministry so that we can attract the wind of the Spirit into our sails?

We Prophesy in Part

In 1 Corinthians 13:9, Paul makes an important statement: *"For we know in part and we prophesy in part."* All prophetic words speak to only a part of our lives and circumstances. It is important that we don't throw away any previous prophetic words that we have received. This latest word may be different from others because the Lord is providing revelation for a different part of our lives.

Where we are unsure about prophecy but feel that the spirit behind it is good, we may need to put it on a shelf and wait. We should encourage all Christians to have a "Holy Spirit shelf" in their lives where they can put things that they don't understand. It may be that, further down the line, they can work it out. They can pray in the meantime and keep taking it down off the shelf, blowing the dust off of it, and bringing it before the Lord.

Some prophecies have fallen off my own shelf altogether. They were given by well-meaning people but actually produced nothing in real terms. The Holy Spirit will always bring things that He has spoken to us back to our memory by way of revelation through Scripture or prophecy. This is not a problem with God, and we can afford to be gracious to people.

Prophecy can be in part, sometimes because of mixture — part man, part God. The revelation was of God, but the interpretation maybe had too many human insights. Prophecy speaks a part word into an area of our lives that God wants to stimulate. That's why God speaks to us: He is speaking to a part of our lives that He wants to encourage and bring into life. This partial word, however, may not speak to the area that we want! God knows what He is doing, and He speaks this prophetic word into the part of our lives that He wants to quicken right now.

Prophecy speaks to the part that the Lord seeks to change

I once prophetically told a man that he needed to look after his mother, who was a widow, unwell and needing financial assistance. His ministry had come under much attack (his own interpretation) and he was struggling to move in the anointing of previous times.

He was convinced that I would have a word from the Lord regarding the source of the attack and a strategy for turning things around. As it turned out he was correct, though not in the way that he envisioned.

The Lord had shown me that because of his treatment of his mother he was not able to partake of the favor of the Lord. It was present, but his behavior was placing a restriction on his ability to realize the blessing. Scripture is clear in this regard.

> *Honor your father and your mother, as the LORD your God has commanded you, that your days may be prolonged and that it may go well with you on the land which the LORD your God gives you. (Deuteronomy 5:16)*

> *Honor your father and mother (which is the first commandment with a promise), so that it may be well with you, and that you may live long on the earth. (Ephesians 6:2–3)*

I used both these Scriptures within the prophetic word as I gave him a strategic guideline of what needed to be done. He accused me of attacking him and wanting to take over his ministry. As the only child, his mother was his responsibility. He was too busy doing the Lord's work as he understood it. He went away, convinced that I not only had missed it but that I was attempting to use prophecy to take over his work. He was disappointed. So was I. Many people miss the opportunities of God to be taken in a higher dimension of relationship and power. They are well disguised. Humility is a low door, which we enter on our knees. Beyond it is a wide and spacious place of blessing and favor. It is impossible to be exalted by God without first being humbled by Him. The greater the humbling, the stronger the exaltation and the bigger possibility of holding onto this new level of anointing. Humility guarantees everything.

We always need to keep our hearts open. We cannot afford to let a sense of disappointment come into our spirits. We need to let this new area that God is looking at receive prayer and attention. God may be opening up an area of life that He wants to deal with. If God wants to deal with a part of our life, we need to let Him in right away. If God wants to touch an issue and we don't let Him, we go around the wilderness one more time and come back to that very same point, that very same issue, that very same place. Like Israel at Kadesh Barnea, we come back to the very first place, but this time it will cost a little bit more to put things right. Why? Because we have had a season of disobedience or whatever it is. The problem has become more entrenched in our lives and it is going to be that much more difficult to move.

There is inflation in truth, and so we must face what God wants to do now and let Him deal with our lives. If we don't, we go around the desert one more time. God is open to reason! He may not change, but He is happy to talk with us. As Isaiah prophesied, "*Come now, and let us reason together... though your sins are as scarlet, they will be as white as snow; though they are red like crimson, they will be like wool.*" (Isaiah 1:18)

If prophecy is partial in content it will also be partial in context. What part of our work or life is this prophecy speaking into? Many times God will be vague on the whole but explicit on a particular part of our life or the work we represent. Take the word and apply it to the part that is under review and learn to cooperate with the Holy Spirit in making necessary adjustments.

Types of Words

All prophecy will normally fall into one of four types. We may even find that a word contains elements of all four: *now, confirming, future,* and *new.*

A *now* word addresses our current life and ministry. It may refer to the past, but it has implications for the present. It may provide us with an agenda for change and can be used as a catalyst for other people to minister into our lives. Remember, prophecy always provides us with some kind of agenda to work and pray through.

Truth costs more when it is ignored

This is why it is so important that we share the prophetic word we have received with mature people. Prophecy is never a matter of personal interpretation. It may require other people to see the things that we cannot see for ourselves and help us through. A now word stimulates the area that God wants to work in at this moment. Lack of response could mean our lives going on hold for a while until we allow the Holy Spirit to have His way.

A *confirming* word will establish and strengthen people in what they know to be right. Continual use of a gift can blunt it. In these circumstances, prophecy is used to "sharpen" people again. People can become legitimately tired in the work. However, without some form of prophetic encouragement or confirmation, they may become tired of the work. I gave a word to one friend that was simply, "Carry on doing on earth what in heaven you are famous for." This brought a renewal of joy and faith that released new strength and confidence in that person to continue the work he was doing. A confirming word builds faith because people know they are in the center of God's will for their lives. It brings a fresh initiative and impetus to fight the enemy. It gives new heart and perspective in the slog of life.

Then there is a *future* word which speaks about the next phase, or next few stages, of our lives. It gives us context and meaning to what we are going through now and what we are to encounter next. It has that essential link with the present that will tie it in effectively to our lives. Although speaking about the future, it has a sense of "fit" within the present.

A future word may map out a particular course as well as help us to see that we are on course right now. It may contain suggestions for training and development, or areas of preparation that need to be considered to meet the demands of the next phase.

It can be given in the present tense. For example, Gideon received a prophetic word that related to his future in Judges 6:12, although the angel of the Lord spoke it in the present tense: "The LORD is with you, O valiant warrior!" At that point, Gideon was hiding and feeling anything but valiant. However, as he responded to God, it actually became his real experience. God's view of the future is not the same as ours. His view though is just as sure and just as certain as the present tense in which He speaks, because He sees the end from the beginning. When God speaks, it is an event; it is a creative word that causes an event to happen.

There are varieties of gift, ministry and effect in prophecy (1 Cor. 12:4–6)

Finally, we have a *new* word. The Lord has things in His heart for us that have never entered our minds. We could never think or imagine it at all (1 Corinthians 2:9–10). It opens up new areas and creates opportunities for us to serve God in other ways.

It is different from a future word in that a new word may have little or no link with the present. Sometimes it can be so far off into the future that it can be difficult for us to comprehend it. In 1973 and 1974, I received several prophetic words that said I would one day raise up prophets all over the world and speak prophetically to kings and governments. At that time, not only had I never prophesied, I didn't even know what prophecy was! I had never encountered the gift. However, within six months, I had begun to prophesy. Twelve years after that prophecy, I began running prophetic schools in the United Kingdom. Today, I do prophetic conferences all across the globe and have spoken prophetically to prime ministers and people in high places.

Initially, the prophetic word was beyond my wildest imagination. I could not conceive it in my mind or heart. Yet it shaped the direction of my life from that point on.

Prophecy opens up new horizons; it provides us with a long-term aim. We can use the prophecy like a compass heading to keep us on track and in the will of God. It will provoke us into seeking the Lord, requesting discipleship, and pushing us into areas of training and preparation. Ultimately, it provides us with a long-term vision that breeds a certain restraint into our lives. We cannot do other things because we have a particular vision, rooted in the prophetic, shaping our lives.

For years, I drove from England to Wales one evening a month to be in the home of Graham Perrins, an anointed prophet and Bible teacher. Those times of study and prayer were well worth the 250 mile round trip in one evening. Graham gave me deep love for Scripture and Bible exposition. I was the quietest member of the group, but I would like to think that I have done a great deal with what Graham taught. I soaked up everything he said like a sponge, took it away, and pondered it closely. Never did I just take notes and file them away at home. I worked everything through each month and came back for more. Graham was, and still is, regarded by me as a father figure in my training on the prophetic.

Obviously, there are overlaps between all the categories, especially between a now and confirming word and a future and new word. Some prophecies can contain elements of all four.

Permission

Our priority is to ask the Lord "What are you saying to me?" Or as Samuel was instructed to say, "Speak, for Your servant is listening." (1 Samuel 3:10)

We may have to determine some things at this time. Is this personal? Is it for someone else here? Is it for the whole church? Is it correctional, directional, or simply inspirational? What type of word is it? A now word? A future one? If it is a confirming word, then what is it authenticating? Is it a new word? Does it fit with the meeting? Does it cut across the meeting? Does it have any negative element or warning? There are many things to think about here. The crucial question that will often override all of the others is "Do I have permission to speak now?"

Prophecy always has an outcome in line with God's loving purpose for us (Jeremiah 29:11)

On numerous occasions the power of the Holy Spirit has come up on me in my own congregation, sometimes so strongly I can barely stand up. The Spirit has begun showing me several things; sometimes there has been a complete understanding, at other times a partial revelation for the church. On many occasions, the Lord did not give me permission to speak that word in that meeting.

Sometimes He wanted me to go away and pray about the revelation for several days or weeks. At other times, the revelation birthed a time of fasting and intercession for the situation. I never got to speak some prophetic words, because my job at the time was to intercede only. Prophecy always gives us a prayer agenda.

On some occasions, I have received a strong prophetic revelation in my own church but had no freedom to speak. Several weeks later, after much prayer, I delivered that same word to another church, thousands of miles away. It exactly fitted that church's circumstances. If we move out solely on the basis of something we feel or because we have few phrases or a picture, we may end up in front of a microphone with precious little to say. To cover our embarrassment, we may turn to volume or repetition to pad out our "word" and make it more acceptable.

This usually results in individuals talking subjectively about how they feel. The prophecy becomes weak as it moves into a more emotional dimension. We ourselves are in the grip of something powerful, but we cannot articulate at this point what we are seeing or feeling. It could simply be a matter of timing and not having sought permission to speak. The prophecy floats over the heads of the church members and never finds a home, leaving them confused and us discouraged. All the while, the Lord may simply be saying to us, "I want to speak to you — come aside!"

There are times when the Lord wants to develop the other side of your prophetic gift, namely intercession. He gives us words that are not intended for man or meetings. They are given to enable us to develop our gifting on our knees in the throne room. We take these words before God and we pray them in to being. We have an outcome prophetically that we can turn into a crafted prayer in His presence.

We join with Jesus who always lives to intercede for us at the right hand of the Father. We learn the discipline of intercession. We learn the secret place of humility before the Lord. All real prophets learn that 80 percent of their anointing is spent on their face before God either in intimate worship, focused meditation, or intercessory prayer. So much of my own ministry is non-public. The greater part of my success in ministry is non-public and extremely personal before the throne.

When God speaks to us prophetically we have to inquire about the next step. Do we have permission to speak to men or do we speak into the face of God Himself? Sometimes there is a subtle and elegant test here that touches our motives and ambitions. The Lord may give us an incredible word that may either put us on the map prophetically or establish our reputation as a prophet. However the Father may want us to deny our selves and forego the acclamation of the church in order to be with Him in ministry. At least we must continue to request permission to speak and really listen to the answer.

We have all had situations where someone has spoken "prophetically" and a spirit of "naffness" has descended on the meeting, causing embarrassment. For the uninitiated, the word naff is an old English expression indicating that something with a high cringe factor has taken place. This is weak prophecy. Usually it occurs towards the end of a meeting and causes confusion. I suggest that perhaps this last-minute prophecy, which failed to accomplish anything, may actually be a word that we use to begin next week's meeting. In the intervening period, we have a week to pray, polish the word, and discuss it with the leaders. Rather than educating the whole church, leaders included, about prophetic protocol, all we see now is platform policemen whose main role is to discourage oddball prophecies from being heard.

In distinguishing between false and poor prophecy delivered by immature gifting, we should not make the mistake of rejecting a prophecy because of the vessel that brought it. Our embarrassment at the method of prophetic delivery should not deter us from hearing the truth it may contain. It is a well-known fact that the enemy will use all means possible to prevent us from receiving input from the mouth and heart of God.

Subsidiary testing helps us to shape the mouthpiece as well as the prophecy. We intend to produce people who can hear accurately and deliver properly the prophetic word.

Conclusion

The world today desperately needs a prophetic church. In times of national crises, the only person we can fully trust is God. There are all kinds of voices out there in the world today and most of them will lead us down the road into death and destruction.

We need to hear the voice of the Lord. To get to that place of reliance on Him, we need purity in our own hearts and lives. God must be able to trust us with words that could affect the course of cities and nations.

Before we see prophets raised up to national prominence, churches need to be raised up to be a prophetic voice in their own community. We need to know what God wants to do in our neighborhoods, our towns, our cities, our regions, and our nations. We need prophetic churches that will be prophetic communities — to live, pray, and speak things into being. We need to anticipate the future because if we don't, we will have the future taken away from us by someone else.

The prophetic enables us to think outside the box of our own spirituality, denominations, and church circles. The prophetic is a kingdom voice, not just a church one — and we badly need it in this day and age. We need to discern the truth from the false and the wise from the ignorant.

I believe that the more prophecy we have in a church, the more evangelism we can do. The church should be pastoring the unsaved into the kingdom, not staring at its own bellybutton for years on end. We need to get out there and serve the Lord. In the midst of that, God will speak to us. Do we know what God wants to do next, evangelistically, in our community?

I used to be part of a team of prophets that did door-to-door evangelism. But we were smart about it and never went to every single door. We didn't want to be rejected ninety-nine times out of a hundred.

Instead, we knocked on the doors where God told us He was doing something. We would send a number of individual intercessors down a street to ask God which families He was working on. If these intercessors all came back with the same house number, we knew God was working there. We could go up to that door with absolute confidence that God was going to do something incredible. He would show us amazing things, and we would prophesy and gives words of knowledge to those people. Breakthrough was always waiting behind that door.

God is serious about what He is doing. He needs a supernatural community to be raised up. All of us need to be prophesying. Our whole church needs to be capable of it for the future of the world hinges on our ability to communicate God's love.

Notes

Notes

Notes

Evaluating the Prophetic Word

Reflections, Exercises and Assignments

The following exercises are designed with this particular chapter in mind. Please work through them carefully before going on to the next chapter. Take time to reflect on your life journey as well as your prophetic development. Learn to work well with the Holy Spirit and people that God has put around you so that you will grow in grace, humility, and wisdom in the ways of God.

Graham Cooke.

What Constitutes Maturity?

For a river to have power to flow and generate the energy to overcome and move obstacles, it must have depth. This is provided by the riverbed banks, which are not present to contain the water, but to direct it purposefully. Otherwise, instead of a river, there is a delta where the water level is a mile wide and an inch deep!

Without depth there is no power and influence. All prophets and prophecy must have depth in order to produce the weight of word necessary to transform people and situations. A lot of prophecy is shallow and without significance. What makes prophecy powerful and profound is the development of the person speaking.

When we accept the disciplines and the necessary constraints of the office, we discover a level of intentionality that enables us to focus the purposes of God in a direct and deliberate manner. We are working with the Lord. We become integrated with the message of the gospel of the kingdom.

Everything that we do and say develops out of the harmony of God's presence, kingdom purpose, and the increase in growth of the body of Christ on earth.

Within the context of this chapter, you must be willing and able to develop these attributes as a sign of your growing maturity.

- You must know the difference between Old Testament prophets and their New Testament counterparts. Your gifting must operate in a grace context because judgment is suspended in Christ until the day of judgment. Jesus, who is prophet, priest, and king, began a whole new generation of prophetic ministers who now model themselves on His gospel and kingdom purpose. Prophetic maturity will be evidenced in the grace and Christ-likeness that you display.
- A lifestyle of accountability is required to operate at high levels consistently in the Spirit. Seek feedback. Have a hunger for personal input. Love the learning that the Father seeks to bring to your heart and mind. Be teachable. Maintain your own humility at a deep level of grace and truth.
- Cultivate the art of prophesying well. Learn how to express the nature of God through edification, exhortation, and comfort. Practice building people up in your everyday conversations. Learn to see people through the mercy, grace, and loving-kindness of God. Speak with compassion and authority. How you speak prophetically tells people a lot about your current relationship with the Lord.
- Understand the purpose of godly authority and your place within that sphere. Align yourself with Scripture. Develop a good track record with regard to accuracy, humility, and teachability in terms of being

led by the Spirit in prophecy. Learn to maintain confidence allied to meekness (not weakness but strength under control) as you cultivate a servant spirit.

- Know how to receive God's permission to speak. Respect the parameters of church leadership and demonstrate the capacity to challenge any restrictions from the place of relationship and not just function. Earn the right to speak by your Christ-likeness. Be articulate and clear about revealing the heart of the Lord. Deal with your own frustrations; do not put them on someone else.
- Know the signs of manipulation and control. Do not overturn the will of the individual. Test the spirit of your own prophecy. Apply the tests to your own word before you release it. Develop a stronger partnership with your own leadership.
- Learn when to speak to people prophetically and when to pray the word into being through private intercession. Cultivate a desire to spend serious time ministering to the Lord. Progressively increase the time and anointing that you spend with God in worship, meditation, and intercession.

What Constitutes Immaturity?

To witness an adult being childish is embarrassing. To observe arrogance, petulance, and sullen behavior is bad enough in a child. To behold it in a grown up diminishes that individual in the eyes of those who are observing. We can only attest to what is our view.

Immaturity is not paying attention to the whole picture of who you are before God and man. There is maturity in gifting as well as character. Sooner or later if these two do not merge and mesh together, our lack of character will disqualify our place in ministry. Then we can only re-qualify ourselves by putting Christlike behaviors at the top of our "to do" list.

Immaturity is not working on both together. Prophetic immaturity is running off at the mouth from a heart that has not mastered transformation of life. There is grace available to enable us to do both. Humility enables grace to be a joyful experience. Without necessary humility, grace works with discipline to bring chastisement, which while not joyful does produce the peaceable fruit of righteousness.

Not learning the parameters of how prophecy works, how to speak, how to partner with God and others means that we are always going to be green instead of seasoned.

Within the confines of this chapter you must face up to the challenges of ongoing immaturity. Here are the possibilities for your consideration.

- Adolescence in gift and ministry first shows up in the way we live our lives. Non-accountable relationships mean that we develop a life without applying truth to ourselves. We can never be in control of our own accountability without being soft on our own immaturity and carnality.
- Immature people prophesy out of their own lack of grace, mercy, and kindness. When we fail to practice Christ-likeness we prophesy more in line with an Old Testament style of delivery than the new word in Christ. Failure to understand grace and truth causes us to move in a harsh spirit and often an arrogant manner. Truth without love can never declare God's heart.
- Juvenile prophets use the gifts for their own promotion. They tend to be super spiritual people who have an exclusive relationship with God that somehow renders them impervious to correction or challenge. They set themselves up as an oracle, beyond reproach. They are upset when their prophetic input is evaluated and can perceive that as unbelief, disregarding the Lord, or raising your hand against the Lord's anointed.
- Immature prophetic people are revealed by their anger, hardness of heart, unteachable spirit, divisiveness, and ignorance of Scripture.

They have immature relationships often with undeveloped people. They do not seek out mature and tested mentors. They have not cultivated a partnership with leadership and have a spirit that serves themselves rather than the people amongst whom God has placed them.

- Unfinished prophetic people seek a platform for their gift which can only be given to someone who has passed their tests and is seasoned. Untested prophetic people are usually prone to frustration, outbursts of anger, and often have little remorse for their actions. They are prone to justify their poor behavior rather than address it and be transformed. They have a victim mentality when challenged and seek to push accountability away from themselves.
- Immature prophetic people do not upgrade their language and methodology in prophesying. They often remain purely spontaneous in their delivery. As people grow, all languages must change to reflect the growth we are making. Juvenile prophets can be stuck in a time warp and a culture that they started with but that has not progressed to something higher as they journey with the Holy Spirit.
- Adolescent prophetic people seldom build relationships of real worth and value. They fail to understand that one of the major parts of a pastoral calling is to protect the flock. A prophet's calling is to develop the people to a higher place of maturity and ability to walk with God. Both objectives develop best in a partnership of mutual love and respect. Immature prophets work on their own rather than in the godly confines of a team of people dedicated to a common purpose.

ASSIGNMENT ONE

Think of a person around your life at this time who may be struggling with issues of righteousness and relationship with the Lord.

Read and meditate on Psalm 86:5–13 on that person's behalf. Ask the Lord to touch your own heart with His compassion and grace for this individual. Without just quoting the Scriptures or merely paraphrasing them prophetically, how would you use this passage as a foundation to bring encouragement, edification, and comfort?

Here are some questions that will help your deliberations.

1. What can you say that would cause them to see the nature of God and experience His heart for them at this time?

2. What is the objective of God in speaking to them in their present situation? What would He want to achieve?

3. What particular promises is the Father releasing to them now?

4. What specific encouragement can you release to them through this word?

5. What transformation does the Father want to generate in their life through your prophecy?

6. How will you speak the prophecy so that you are in agreement with God's heart?

When you have answered the above questions, use that and the Scripture to put together a prophetic word that accurately represents the heart of the Father and releases the individual into fresh faith and a deeper relationship with the Lord.

ASSIGNMENT TWO

Joy – The Fruit Of The Spirit

Joy is rooted in the character and nature of God. He dwells in everlasting joy. His presence is full of joy, laughter, and rejoicing! God is joyous. Joy is the very atmosphere of heaven.

"On earth as it is in heaven" is always one of the principles within which the Father lives and moves. Therefore, we must continuously experience joy as a way of life because joy is one of the earthly manifestations of God's kingdom.

Joy is who God is; rejoicing is our response to the nature of God. Rejoicing is an outward manifestation to the inward presence of joy. That is why we count all things as joy, because it is such a fruitful way to live. Trials give us greater opportunities to be joyful and rejoice in who God is for us, regardless of circumstances.

The joy of the Lord must go deep if our rejoicing is to take us into a high place of His affection. As spirit-filled believers we are learning how to fill up our inner space with God's presence. We are learning to be of good cheer because God has overcome!

It is imperative that we root ourselves in the Father's absolute delight over us. He rejoices over us with singing. When we accept that joy is God's normal provision for us, then we can learn the art of living every day beneath His smile.

What we see in the face of God we reflect back to Him. He makes us full of gladness with His presence (Acts 2:28). We must properly acknowledge what we've been given or we will not be able to experience that particular reality in Christ. Rejoice because you have joy, not in order to feel joyful!

Joy is a fruit of the Spirit that comes with the personality of the Holy Spirit as He abides in us in Christ. Allowing His personality to transform ours sets us free to know Him in truth and therefore releases us from ourselves to be like Him.

Joy celebrates the nature of God. Knowing God is easier and more wonderful when we allow our hearts to marinate in His essential nature. Joy enables us to pursue and perceive a higher dimension of spiritual reality. We can more readily receive the desires and affections of God. Our hearts become lighter so that our identity and relationship with God can become more glorious.

Joy brings us into the presence of God and connects our inner man to what the Father is saying and doing in our circumstances. Joy establishes our focus and intention on the goodness of God so that our mind is renewed and we perceive kingdom reality. Our awareness of who God is for us causes us to step forward into our situation knowing that God is with us and for us!

Joy releases our ability to magnify God at a higher level than our circumstances. Joy will never allow anything to get bigger than our consciousness of

God. It is in our DNA to magnify. It is how we were created. If we do not magnify the Lord, rest assured, we will magnify something! We could magnify the circumstances, the enemy, our own weakness, human opposition — just to name a few.

Joy releases divine expectation because it enables us to stay close to God's ability to do the impossible. We become filled with His radical love and delight over us. Joy cancels any negative thought processes. We are empowered to focus on the greatness and goodness of God on our personal behalf. Joy creates an opportunity for us to be strengthened by God, massively encouraged.

It is impossible for us to be depressed or discouraged when we are filled with an awareness of God's innate happiness!

1. What is standing between you and an experience of the Father's joy?

2. How does this particular aspect of God's nature most inspire you in your relationship with Him?

3. What priority are you going to put on receiving a greater revelation of God's joy over you, and why?

4. What current circumstances are robbing you of joy and how will you overturn that dilemma?

5. How do you think the Father will use joy to bring a breakthrough in your current situation?

6. How will you cooperate with God in this regard?

7. What must change in you for you to become more joyful and to have a lifestyle characterized by joy?

CASE STUDY

Matching prophetic delivery with content

The delivery of a prophetic word must match its content. One cannot shout into a person's face that the Lord is giving them rest and peace. Likewise a prophecy about courage and warrior strength cannot be delivered in a nervous stutter.

The context determines what God wants to say and the method of delivery must be in line with God's heart so that the content of the message is fully heard and received as God intended.

Study the following prophecy and answer the questions following it.

> *Megan, I see a picture of you running joyfully at speed carrying a huge red heart many times bigger than you. You are laughing and shouting for joy, running fast but totally unable to see where you are going.*
>
> *It is a picture of how you are going to journey with the heart of God in these coming years. There is no fear in your life whatsoever — just an incredible joy and a huge capacity to be totally carefree in God's heart towards you.*
>
> *You will carry God's heart in a huge way. You will be known for it. His heart will always be bigger than any obstacle or opposition. His heart will consume you. You will have a passion to carry the heart of God throughout your life and throughout the world. Everywhere you go the heart of God in you will have a huge impact on the people that you meet.*
>
> *The answer to all your questions and fears will always be for the Father to show you His heart towards you. You will become hugely confident about living in and from the heartbeat of His affection and delight in you.*
>
> *Your own heart will be transformed. You shall come to a place in God's delight where you will never know fear again, for you will be constantly overwhelmed at the fullness of His heart for you.*
>
> *You will minister His heart to people and cause breakthroughs wherever you go. You will not be at all concerned that you cannot see the way ahead. Yours is a unique anointing to be able to see into the heart of God in such a way that you will become most confident in who He is for you at all times.*

1. What is the crux of this word?

2. What is the emotion and plan of God for Megan?

3. What is the best way to deliver this word to her? (How would the Father say it to Megan?)

4. After giving the word, what would you pray over Megan to seal her into the experience of it?

LECTIO DIVINA

Lectio Divina (Latin for *divine reading*) is an ancient way of reading the Bible, allowing a quiet and contemplative way of coming to God's Word. *Lectio Divina* opens the pulse of the Scripture, helping readers dig far deeper into the Word than normally happens in a quick glance-over.

In this exercise, we will look at a portion of Scripture and use a modified *Lectio Divina* technique to engage it. This technique can be used on any piece of Scripture; I highly recommend using it for key Bible passages that the Lord has highlighted for you, and for anything you think might be an inheritance word for your life (see the Crafted Prayer interactive journal for more on inheritance words).

Read the Scripture

> *Then He said to me, "Son of man, eat what you find; eat this scroll, and go, speak to the house of Israel."*
>
> *So I opened my mouth, and He fed me this scroll.*
>
> *He said to me, "Son of man, feed your stomach and fill your body with this scroll which I am giving you." Then I ate it, and it was sweet as honey in my mouth.*
>
> *Then He said to me, "Son of man, go to the house of Israel and speak with My words to them. For you are not being sent to a people of unintelligible speech or difficult language, but to the house of Israel, nor to many peoples of unintelligible speech or difficult language, whose words you cannot understand. But I have sent you to them who should listen to you; yet the house of Israel will not be willing to listen to you, since they are not willing to listen to Me. Surely the whole house of Israel is stubborn and obstinate. Behold, I have made your face as hard as their faces and your forehead as hard as their foreheads. Like emery harder than flint I have made your forehead. Do not be afraid of them or be dismayed before them, though they are a rebellious house."*
>
> *Moreover, He said to me, "Son of man, take into your heart all My words which I will speak to you and listen closely. Go to the exiles, to the sons of your people, and speak to them and tell them, whether they listen or not, 'Thus says the* LORD GOD.*' "*
>
> *Then the Spirit lifted me up, and I heard a great rumbling sound behind me, "Blessed be the glory of the* LORD *in His place."*
>
> *And I heard the sound of the wings of the living beings touching one another and the sound of the wheels beside them, even a great rumbling*

sound. So the Spirit lifted me up and took me away; and I went embittered in the rage of my spirit, and the hand of the LORD was strong on me. Then I came to the exiles who lived beside the river Chebar at Telabib, and I sat there seven days where they were living, causing consternation among them.

At the end of seven days the word of the LORD came to me, saying, "Son of man, I have appointed you a watchman to the house of Israel; whenever you hear a word from My mouth, warn them from Me. When I say to the wicked, 'You will surely die,' and you do not warn him or speak out to warn the wicked from his wicked way that he may live, that wicked man shall die in his iniquity, but his blood I will require at your hand. Yet if you have warned the wicked and he does not turn from his wickedness or from his wicked way, he shall die in his iniquity; but you have delivered yourself. Again, when a righteous man turns away from his righteousness and commits iniquity, and I place an obstacle before him, he will die; since you have not warned him, he shall die in his sin, and his righteous deeds which he has done shall not be remembered; but his blood I will require at your hand. However, if you have warned the righteous man that the righteous should not sin and he does not sin, he shall surely live because he took warning; and you have delivered yourself."

The hand of the LORD was on me there, and He said to me, "Get up, go out to the plain, and there I will speak to you." So I got up and went out to the plain; and behold, the glory of the LORD was standing there, like the glory which I saw by the river Chebar, and I fell on my face.

The Spirit then entered me and made me stand on my feet, and He spoke with me and said to me, "Go, shut yourself up in your house. As for you, son of man, they will put ropes on you and bind you with them so that you cannot go out among them. Moreover, I will make your tongue stick to the roof of your mouth so that you will be mute and cannot be a man who rebukes them, for they are a rebellious house. But when I speak to you, I will open your mouth and you will say to them, 'Thus says the Lord GOD.' He who hears, let him hear; and he who refuses, let him refuse; for they are a rebellious house." (Ezekiel 3)

1. Find a place of stillness before God. Embrace His peace. Chase the nattering thoughts out of your mind. Calm your body. Breathe slowly. Inhale. Exhale. Inhale. Exhale. Clear yourself of the distractions of life. Whisper the word, "Stillness." Take your time. When you find that rest in the Lord, enjoy it. Worship Him in it. Be with Him there.

2. Reread the passage twice. Allow its words to become familiar to you. Investigate Ezekiel's call. What images does that bring to your spirit? What do you see? Become a part of it. What phrases or words especially resonate with you? Meditate especially on those shreds of revelation. Write those pieces down in your journal.

3. Read the passage twice again. Like waves crashing onto a shore, let the words of Scripture crash onto your spirit. What excites you? What scares you? What exhilarates you about this revelation of the nature of God? What are you discerning? What are you feeling? What are you hearing? Again, write it all down in your journal.

4. Write the theme of this passage in your journal.

5. Does this passage rekindle any memories or experiences? Does it remind you of any prophetic words you have given or received? Write those down as well.

6. What is the Holy Spirit saying to you through this Scripture? Investigate it with Him — picture the two of you walking through it together. Write those words in your journal.

7. Read the passage two final times. Meditate on it. Is there something God wants you to do? Is there something He is calling you to? Write it down.

8. Pray silently. Tell God what this passage is saying to you. Tell Him what you are thinking about. Write down your conversation together. Picture yourself and the Holy Spirit as two old friends in a coffee shop, chatting about what God is doing.

9. Finally, pray and thank God for His relationship with you. Come back to the passage once a week for the next three months. Read it and let more revelation flow into you. If you feel compelled to, craft a prayer based on this passage for yourself, your family, your friends, or church. Pray that prayer until you feel God has birthed it in you.

Notes

Notes

Notes

Notes

MODULE THREE

HANDLING WRONG PROPHECY

MODULE THREE

Handling Wrong Prophecy

WHAT YOU WILL LEARN IN THIS SEGMENT:

- The different stages of relationship with God as we move towards maturity.
- Creating a safe environment in church where people are free to experience, experiment, and learn.
- Turning personal insecurity into a joyful vulnerability before God.
- Learning how to grow up in God.
- How to get free and stay free!
- Developing a childlike simplicity.
- Developing a proper relationship with the Holy Spirit.
- The meaning and purpose of frustration.
- How to be a catalyst for change.
- To develop opportunities in the Spirit.
- The difference between false and poor prophecy.
- The relationship between spontaneity and planned prophecy.
- How to turn mistakes into a positive learning experience.
- The elements of poor prophecy.
- The aspects of excellent prophecy.
- The difference between being children of God and becoming sons of God.
- Handling wrong prophecy.
- Handling wrong prophecy in a meeting context.
- Creating an environment that welcomes prophecy.
- The principles of accountability.

MODULE THREE

Handling Wrong Prophecy

INEVITABLY, PEOPLE MAKE MISTAKES and extend beyond their measure in prophecy. When we are developing ministry and gifting, we need to create an environment where people are free to fail. If we insist on perfection or maturity in the early stages of development, we will not cultivate people in the right manner.

Instead of faith to explore the prophetic, we will cause a fear that will hold back. Instead of boldness, we will create intimidation. Rather than producing mature men and women, we cause their gifts and ministries to level off. That ceiling will be the measure of our disapproval at their inexperience and our unwillingness to see that discipleship involves loving correction.

Growing people will cause us hard work and some heartache, but people are worth the hassle. We must cultivate the attitude in our churches that people have worth and value. Helping people mature is a biblical mandate. In Scripture, writers used four different stages to show how a person must mature spiritually: *nepios* (baby), *teknon* (child), *paidion* (adolescent), and *huios* (mature son or daughter).

Development instead of punishment

I still remember the attendant feelings and emotions that I had when I first moved out in the supernatural many years ago. I was a child in what I knew. I was awestruck, afraid, uncertain, insecure, and inadequate. Like a toddler tripping over his own feet, I prophesied. I was convinced that I had done everything all wrong. I felt stupid when I could not properly verbalize what I was sensing. I felt like everyone was laughing at my mistakes.

I remember, too, the awful pride that I went through as I became more accustomed to speaking and moving in supernatural ways. Like a moody teenager who thinks they know everything, I fell into arrogance.

When we look back at our early development, I imagine most of us cringe at the mistakes we made. I was so desperate for approval, kindness, and, above all, real help in my development.

People need to be free to make mistakes and to fail. Our leaders must create an environment within the church that is safe for both the body and the developing prophet. Once we set a protocol for prophetic ministry to follow and appoint someone to oversee that area, we can genuinely relax. Prophetic protocol teaches us how to use revelational prophecy and the accountability required. We can sow that teaching into our foundational classes and ministry training. We can then determine what are honest mistakes needing loving correction, and what are breaches of protocol that may require discipline and adjustment.

We must learn to deal with failures and turn them into positive learning experiences for people. We cannot simply drop people or forbid them to prophesy; we must work with them to overcome their difficulties. We should be kind, humble, and full of mercy — yet firm, caring, and well-disciplined. The leader's role is to balance care for the individual with protection for the flock. We are not employers; we cannot fire people from their gift. We cannot dismiss their life and ministry because they create tension and difficulty. People are worth fighting for and therefore, our heart is always to win people.

The grace of God abounds when sin is plentiful. We need the same godly reaction to failure. Our love, warmth, and acceptance needs to abound. People need us most when they have failed. It is not easy to begin to move in the supernatural; it is full of pressure and uncertainty until we develop proper practice. We learn mostly by experience, and that is costly to acquire. Often we learn how not to do things before figuring out how to do them properly. We should respect and be grateful for anyone willing to put himself in that kind of firing line. Whenever a person begins to move in the supernatural, he may as well paint a big target on his back and yell "Shoot me!" Developing prophets draws enemy attacks and Christian criticism. Church people should set their sights on redemption, not harassment.

Turn failure into a positive learning experience

I need my brothers and sisters more when I have failed than I do when I have succeeded. Success should bring approval while failure should bring acceptance. To do otherwise is to be worldly and not godly.

Baby Steps

The four stages of spiritual maturity are directly linked to how developing prophetic ministries operate. When we first come to Christ, we are babies in the faith. The Greek word *nepios* was used by Paul in 1 Corinthians 3:1–3 to describe baby Christians: *"And I, brethren, could not speak to you as to spiritual men, but as to men of flesh, as to infants in Christ. I gave you milk to drink, not solid food; for you were not yet able to receive it. Indeed, even now you are not yet able, for you are still fleshly. For since there is jealousy and strife among you, are you not fleshly, and are you not walking like mere men?"*

Young believers can and should enjoy this stage, as it is an important first step when we are born again. As a *nepios,* we learn how to live in the loving kindness of God. We also learn how to become more and more vulnerable to God, a process that actually matures us in our faith. The more vulnerable we are to God, the less vulnerable we are to ourselves. We mature greatly the first time we realize that we cannot do anything ourselves. It is like a baby's first step — our world changes. When we come to God and say, "I can't do this alone, I'm no good," He gets a twinkle in His eye. "I know," He answers, "that's why I chose you. You be who you are, and I'll be who I am, and together, we'll change the world."

However, we cannot live in the *nepios* stage for the rest of our Christian lives. Eventually, we must begin to chew the solid food of our faith. It is very difficult to be around someone who has been a Christian for twenty years but is still a baby. These overgrown babies live in a needs-driven manner.

Babies are attention-seeking. They don't care who they disturb or when they disturb them. They kick up a fuss until they get their needs met. They need constant reassurance. With a new Christian, such hard work is well worth it. But with someone who has been saved for a long time, it is an unnecessary and unhealthy headache.

> *Personal insecurity must turn into a joyful vulnerability in God's goodness*

Spiritual babies live by their soulish senses, not by any sense of spiritual perception. Life is guided by what they feel, what they think, and what they want. None of this is wrong initially, but we cannot live like that long-term. Eventually, each of us has to win the battle of faith versus feelings, because God calls us to walk by faith, not sight or feelings. As we learn to do this, our feelings learn how to be inspired by God. We start to distinguish the first slivers of revelation, like a baby saying "dada" for the first time. We learn rudimentary spiritual language and truth.

"*When I was a child, I used to speak like a child, think like a child, reason like a child; when I became a man, I did away with childish things,*" Paul wrote in 1 Corinthians 13:11. This is the test before every baby Christian. "*We are no longer to be children, tossed here and there by waves and carried about by every wind of doctrine, by the trickery of men, by craftiness in deceitful scheming; but speaking the truth in love, we are to grow up in all aspects into Him who is the head, even Christ,*" Paul added in Ephesians 4:14–15.

Every single stage of growing up in God should be enjoyed. If you are a young Christian, having been saved less than a couple of years, you will identify with certain *nepios* characteristics. It takes time to grow up, start walking, learn how to feed ourselves, and learn how to clean ourselves. But it is a great day when we can do these things for ourselves, and trust the affirmation of the Holy Spirit to be our great guide and encouragement.

Nepios revelation is simple, inspirational, and always for the individual themselves. It is a small step in their journey toward Christian maturity.

Childish Behavior

The second stage in our journey toward spiritual maturity is the child, or *teknon*, stage. While *nepios* babies don't know many of the basics of the faith, *teknon* children know them but don't fully practice them.

Developing Christians need constant instruction in right living. When we know someone who is in the early stages of walking with God, or in moving in the prophetic, we must preach the same truths to them over and over. What are the most important things they need to know and develop? These are the messages we need to state and restate. We have to keep reinforcing the truth until it becomes second nature to them.

When we have children, we teach them basics that will help them stay safe. "Don't talk to strangers," we say again and again, until it sinks in. It is no different for spiritual children. We must teach the same lesson many times.

The early Church operated this way. Without any New Testament Scripture, they memorized Christ's teachings by repeating them over and over. No wonder Jesus boiled down the entire Bible to just two statements: "You shall love the LORD your God with all your heart, and with all your soul, and with all your strength, and with all your mind," and "[love] your neighbor as yourself," (Luke 10:27). Because most people, including the apostles, were illiterate, church leaders had to focus on the basics. Still, with a practical theology and a great experience of the Holy Spirit they turned the world upside down.

Teknons need to be instructed in the basics as well. The apostle John understood this, as we see in 1 John 2:1–12:

> *My little children, I am writing these things to you so that you may not sin. And if anyone sins, we have an Advocate with the Father, Jesus Christ the righteous; and He Himself is the propitiation for our sins; and not for ours only, but also for those of the whole world.*
>
> *By this we know that we have come to know Him, if we keep His commandments. The one who says, "I have come to know Him," and does not keep His commandments, is a liar, and the truth is not in him; but whoever keeps His word, in him the love of God has truly been perfected.*
>
> *By this we know that we are in Him: the one who says he abides in Him ought himself to walk in the same manner as He walked. Beloved, I am not writing a new commandment to you, but an old commandment which you have had from the beginning; the old commandment is the word which you have heard. On the other hand, I am writing a new commandment to you, which is true in Him and in you, because the darkness is passing away and the true Light is already shining. The one who says*

> *he is in the Light and yet hates his brother is in the darkness until now. The one who loves his brother abides in the Light and there is no cause for stumbling in him. But the one who hates his brother is in the darkness and walks in the darkness, and does not know where he is going because the darkness has blinded his eyes.*
>
> *I am writing to you, little children, because your sins have been forgiven you for His name's sake.*

Teknon Christians must learn the importance of unity and love. This should seed every prophecy that is ever given. When we love our brother, we walk in the light of God's revelation. We come to a point where we are no longer preoccupied with ourselves. We begin to look for ways to bless the people around us. The greatest lesson a *teknon* child must learn is that we demonstrate our love for God by how we treat the people around us.

If we do nothing tangibly to help people around us, we are doing very little in our relationship with God. We cannot love God in a vacuum. The best way to keep the enemy away, and keep our spiritual lives vital and blossoming, is to be obedient to the Word of God, to live in the Spirit, and to love the people God has put around us.

Downsides exist in the lives of *teknon*. Children throw tantrums when they don't get their way. Overgrown childish Christians have hidden lifestyles and secret sin. They refuse discipline and true accountability. They want things their way — right or wrong. Their behavior is unpredictable: light one moment, dark the next.

The key to moving *teknon* Christians to the next level is to teach them how to have deep, meaningful friendships. If they love God and love others, they can continue to mature. Many *teknons* have surface relationships instead of deep friendships. We need truth, honesty, and openness to go deep with people.

The truest measure of a *teknon* Christian is that they can win a battle to get free, but lose the one to stay free. Most people can win the first battle to get out of a particular habit or sin, but three months later, they have lost the second fight and have slipped back into the same bad pattern.

> *One battle to get free, another battle to stay free!*

We have the capacity, through our relationship with the Holy Spirit, to break through and win battles. We can sustain that breakthrough. But the difference between a *teknon* and a mature Christian is that *teknons* waver when they cannot feel the presence of God. Mature, or *huios,* Christians know that God's presence is not just a feeling. *Teknons* have moments of great glory and victory, but then slip. They end up losing ground and coming back to the point where the Lord has to touch them again; most people think this is normal Christianity.

We grow in our relationship with God through obedience, loving the truth, and loving other people — not through other Christians laying hands on us and praying for a miraculous breakthrough. While I love such breakthroughs, people cannot become dependent on those things to get free and stay free because God has laid out a better way to live. We need to teach *teknons* how to live in the Spirit. When we become obedient and practice the truth, we don't need others to babysit us any more. We come to church to contribute something, not just to receive ministry.

As with *nepios* Christians, being a *teknon* is not a bad thing in season. People who have been saved for just a few years should be ravenous for the things of God. They should soak up His truth and life like a sponge. Just as children learn to read and do other important, everyday tasks, so a *teknon* should be growing in the basics of the faith. There is a wonderful, childlike simplicity that *teknon* Christians should hold on to at all costs. Curiosity is an important part of the learning process. *Teknon* Christians should enjoy discovering God, their spiritual gifts, and how to use them.

It is in this stage that we must begin to develop our lifestyle of accountability. Initially this is best done by asking questions, seeking advice, and practicing the gift in front of other people. Love the learning involved in every situation and growth will be continuous.

Lose your fear of making mistakes by developing a partnership with someone who is ahead of you in experience. You will make mistakes; learn to face them calmly and honorably. Delight in the process of discovery regarding the heart and nature of God.

Spotty Adolescents

The third stage of spiritual maturity is adolescence, or *paidion*. Jesus used this form of the word children to describe the Pharisees, the spiritual leaders of His day, in Luke 7:30–35:

> *But the Pharisees and the lawyers rejected God's purpose for themselves, not having been baptized by John. To what then shall I compare the men of this generation, and what are they like?*
>
> *They are like children who sit in the market place and call to one another, and they say, "We played the flute for you, and you did not dance; we sang a dirge, and you did not weep." For John the Baptist has come eating no bread and drinking no wine, and you say, "He has a demon!" The Son of Man has come eating and drinking, and you say, "Behold, a gluttonous man and a drunkard, a friend of tax collectors and sinners!"*
>
> *Yet wisdom is vindicated by all her children.*

Jesus' Pharisaical counterparts were like spotty teenagers. They were completely wrapped up in their own ministries and agendas, and unable to bend to what God was doing. They rejected the obvious prophetic sign and life of John the Baptist, and missed the gateway to understanding Christ.

Sadly, many ministries are still *paidion* in their maturity. I have known people who have been in international ministry for fifteen years but are still teenagers in their spiritual maturity. Like the Pharisees ignoring the flute and mourning around them, these people are obsessed with their own ministry and revelation. Conversations with individuals like this are always one-way; they share their vision and don't bother asking about yours.

But Jesus didn't only call the Pharisees *paidions*. After His resurrection, He visited the sea shore and watched as His disciples struggled to catch fish. Peter and his friends were demoralized after Jesus' trial and crucifixion. With no where else to turn, these men, who had lived with Jesus for three years and seen the kind of miracles we would give our eye teeth for, went back to their old lives and professions. They had given up in the face of adversity.

In John 21, Jesus called that behavior adolescent. Immature Christians give up when the going gets tough. They let go of their experiences with God in the face of adversity. Certainly, the disciples were on their way to spiritual maturity, but they hadn't made it yet. They were older than *nepios* babies, but still only half-formed. It is better to be an adolescent than a baby after ten years in church, but we cannot get stuck in any phase of life.

Teenagers know how to do certain things. Christian *paidions* have had experiences with God and walked with Him for some length of time. They have had some profound times, but they are still learning the true nature of the Holy Spirit.

It is not the Holy Spirit's job to make things easy for us. His role is actually to walk with us through every step of our journey. He will be whatever we need. Sometimes, He is our instructor, while at other times He is our comforter. If the Holy Spirit's mission was to make life easy, we wouldn't need a comforter. In Acts 9, we read of how the early church walked in the fear of the Lord and the comfort of the Holy Spirit.

> *Adversity should prove who you are in Jesus!*

A major transition occurs in the life of a *paidion* when they discover what God meant when He promised to never leave nor forsake us. They realize that only the comfort of the Spirit protects them from the fear of the Lord. They open their hearts to the Holy Spirit, allowing Him to teach them how to endure what is happening around them.

The Pharisees never learned that lesson, but fortunately the disciples did. The apostles allowed God to be whatever He wanted to be for them as individuals and as a Church. The Pharisees, however, never broke out of the *paidion* issue of always doing something but never learning how to be. One of the great problems of a *paidion* in ministry is that they are preoccupied with their work at the expense of their relationship with Christ. They take ministry over fellowship and end up being half-formed in their relationships with God and people.

The frightening thing about a *paidion* is that they can often carry a powerful anointing but do not have the character to sustain their relationship with Jesus. They are giants in public but poisoned dwarves in private. People who know them well find it difficult to reconcile what they say on stage with how they act behind closed doors.

Paidions and Frustration

Relationships are always a key issue in the spiritual development of people. Often frustration occurs because people feel they are unheard or unloved. Yes, some people are difficult to love. However they must still be listened to. If people feel rejected, they may speak out of that emotion. Friendship reduces the tension that people can feel around their lives.

When frustration is present in the life of an individual, they will probably see and hear God correctly but interpret it in a completely wrong way. They are ruled, however slightly, by emotions, perceptions, and situations. An edge is added to their prophecy that is unhelpful. This is a very common problem among *paidion* prophetic ministries. We all remember how, as teenagers, we were ruled by our own perceptions, angst, and hormones. A spiritual teenager is no different.

Occasionally, immature prophetic people can be found firing the bullets of other people. It is easy for some to be pointed in a certain direction. Leaders need to watch for signs of manipulation and control, either in the person prophesying, or in the people around them. Cliques do form in churches, and we must be aware of the danger of negative fellowship. Of course, this applies to everyone, not just those with a prophetic gifting. It is, however, more dangerous in practice to have prophetic people indulging in such things.

> *God loves our emotions too much to allow them to remain negative!*

People who are frustrated or prophesying their own thoughts need love, patience, and discipline. Find the redemptive key that unlocks their hearts. With every human problem, there is a rescue plan, a redemptive key, to unlock the right response. The Holy Spirit is wonderful at repossession and recovery.

Frustration can also be a sign that people care so much for the church that they cannot see or conceive of anything else. They are driven to distraction. They can feel that things are moving too slowly or that they are missing something vital. They may, of course, be right. That is why our evaluation has to be based on real integrity on our part. Our allegiance is always to the truth.

To understand frustration and the impact it is supposed to have personally and corporately, we must have our heart and mind rooted in an ongoing experience of rest in the Lord: "*Come to Me, all who are weary and heavy-laden, and I will give you rest. Take My yoke upon you and learn from Me, for I am gentle and humble in heart, and you will find rest for your souls. For My yoke is easy and My burden is light.*" (Matthew 11:28–30)

Being weary and heavy laden is having a negative experience of life that is controlling our thoughts, emotions, and actions.

Frustration does not exist in heaven. It is a worldly construct put together by people who do not have a full experience of peace, rest, patience, long-suffering with joy, perseverance, and faithfulness. When we do not practice the fruit of the Spirit, frustration is the result. When we are frustrated over a long period of time we become weary and heavy in our approach to God and life. The antidote to frustration is not the resolution of the problem in front of us. We are the problem. Frustration is a mindset caused by how we view ourselves in the Lord.

Frustration is really discontent

The antidote to frustration is rest and peace. It is to learn patience and faithful stewardship. It is to become some thing more in the Lord. We legitimize our negativity when we give it a name — frustration.

Frustration occurs because we feel checked, opposed, unable to move forward. We blame others, isolate ourselves, and vent our emotions in negative thinking and conversation. We do not deal with our negativity, we give it life. We allow it to remain and fester in our hearts.

Frustration is a sign that God is first dealing with us personally. He is searching our hearts. Frustration is present because patience is not! It reveals a lack of rest and peace and it makes trust more improbable. We must exchange frustration for an experience of rest. Jesus must become our Prince of Peace at a deeper level. If we will allow the Holy Spirit to deal with our negativity, we will hear God differently and be empowered to see what He is doing and desiring. Rest allows us to receive wisdom. Frustration makes wisdom impossible. It binds us into the natural. Rest releases us to soar in the Spirit to a higher level. The view from a place of rest is all encompassing.

Rest is a release from the mental, physical, emotional effects of stress. We cannot function in this war without rest. Walking with God is about working with God, not against Him. His yoke is easy and His burden is light. As it is with Him, so it is with us.

There is gentleness and humility about the Father that causes us to be lifted up and become lighter! There is an ease in being with God that causes us to overcome, as He overcomes. In Isaiah 40:28–31, we read:

> *Do you not know? Have you not heard? The Everlasting God, the* LORD, *the Creator of the ends of the earth does not become weary or tired. His understanding is inscrutable. He gives strength to the weary, and to him who lacks might He increases power. Though youths grow weary and*

tired, and vigorous young men stumble badly, yet those who wait for the LORD will gain new strength; They will mount up with wings like eagles, They will run and not get tired, They will walk and not become weary.

There is a place set aside for us in the Spirit where we can make the enemy tired and weary. Waiting on the Lord involves worshipping, rejoicing, resting, listening, and learning patience. Just settling back into Him. Learning how to be occupied with Him. Being seated with Him in a higher place. The enemy comes to steal, kill, and destroy. He destroys our relationship with the Lord, our true spiritual perspective, our ability to receive wisdom, and our capacity to affect the people around us in the proper manner. He makes life stale. The Holy Spirit refreshes! Power in warfare is concerned with staying fresher longer. It is about abiding in Christ in a way that means we bring a freshness to situations that allows God to move in acceleration.

Frustration is God's catalyst for change

The more rested in God the faster we can move. We need to run in these days because the church is behind the times of her development. We have ground to make up if we are to be on track and in time with God's purpose. We must learn the art of accelerated living and not becoming weary.

Frustration therefore is a catalyst for personal and corporate transformation. We must allow the Holy Spirit to use our frustration effectively, or the enemy will use it as a powerful effect on us and through us. Few people know the difference between frustration and irritation.

Frustration occurs when we are seeing something on one level and are being blocked by another. A plan, a vision that we have in the Spirit is prevented from progressing on the natural level. We feel prevented from doing or achieving some thing that is dear or significant to us.

Irritation is caused out of our carnal capacity to be angry and annoyed at people and circumstances and to believe the worst about someone or something. We can be so easily irritated by someone or something that we have no time for anyway! Constant irritability leads to abnormal sensitivity to self, and we become quickly offended.

If unchecked by patience, love, forbearance, or self control, our frustration will develop as an irritation which will lead us into exasperation and a temper blow out. We chafe. We are rankled, and lack of self control means we vent our anger on someone.

Irritation and the negative emotions that accompany it are a sign where our flesh needs to be touched by the Spirit. It's a sign pointing towards our next transformation! Irritation does not go away. It gets stored, like body fat. This is why we must exercise ourselves to godliness.

Frustration must first bring us to a sense of the goal of God. It must point us to His essential nature and character that He wants us to live in and enjoy throughout this particular trial or situation. The spirit that we act in and speak from will stay with us. So we will either grow in the Spirit or the flesh.

Second, frustration will point towards a greater awareness of destiny and vision unfolding. The next phase of the journey is coming into view. How we travel that road is so vital to our ongoing development. The goal of God is primarily to make each one of us Christlike.

The temptation is always to attach our frustrations to a particular issue or to certain people. We feel thwarted and obstructed and we don't like it. Instead of becoming more like Jesus and operating from a higher place in the Spirit, we descend into a lower state of being. The carnality that is present instead of being dealt with is actually released into the circumstances to wreak havoc. "I feel frustrated because our worship has not been developing. If only they would get out of the way and let the Spirit move, everything would be fine."

Frustration will put us in one camp or another. It will put us into the opposition camp where "they" are the enemy. We have allowed ourselves to be divided and now we can become divisive also. We could use our frustration as God intends — first, to change ourselves and become more like Jesus, and second, to intercede and hear the word of the Lord.

Whoever rules your frustration rules you!

Third, we use it to affect change through partnership with those around us. "They" becomes "we" as relationships go to a new level of intentionality. When we place frustration elsewhere, other than our relationship with the Lord, we do not take responsibility for what is happening. We become victims of frustration rather than catalysts within it! Prophetic people are good at this, unfortunately. We turn what could be blessings and revelation into warnings and judgments.

Because of something within us that has not been dealt with properly, our frustration becomes negative rather than positive. It is now a hindrance rather than the opportunity that God has decreed. We miss the point, miss God, and allow the enemy to work in and through us.

The Holy Spirit gives us a vision of what the church will become next, and we do not encourage the people to look up and press in to God for the future. Instead, out of our negativity we declare, "I have this against you, says the Lord, that you are not this." We can see that the Lord wants to release worship and a new depth of prayer. In our frustration we judge the church because the worship and prayer are substandard. Our frustration is present to enable us to put a foot in the door of opportunity and keep saying the word continuously because we believe that God will move on it. Our frustration is our wake-up call to enable us to serve the Lord as He requires. Some prophecies must be given creatively several times before they are received. It is our joy to repeat God's intentions. Of course, if frustration has hold of us negatively, then joy is the last thing we will be experiencing.

A catalyst is someone who precipitates an event. A real prophet is always alive to a quickening spirit. We are always aware of the possibility of Divine Acceleration. It is the Spirit who quickens (John 6:63; 1 Timothy 6:13). Jesus, the last Adam, was made a quickening spirit. (1 Corinthians 15:45)

The Greek transliteration here is *zoopoieo* (dzo-op-oy-eh-o). It means to "bestow life quickly as in resurrection power; or to revitalize; or the power to reproduce; or the power to change suddenly." It points to the sudden impartation of spiritual life. It bestows an ability to respond to God's voice immediately. Salvation quickens us into a relationship with God. Our response, because we have the indwelling Holy Spirit, can now be "quickened" at any time.

Frustration is meant to create an opportunity

Frustration blocks a quickening. This is why we must allow ourselves to be dealt with first by the Holy Spirit. Paul's injunction was "in me first" (1 Timothy 1:16). That is a terrific example! Prophets look for opportunities to accelerate the church into a new place with the Holy Spirit. They seek to expedite a new season of change and advance. Frustration is the catalyst for change and the agent of increase.

Sometimes it's healthy for prophetic people to come into an experience of their own prophecy *before* they give it to the church. Then we are speaking out of a known place of revelatory experience. The word is living and active and can cause a quickening. The prophecy is authentic in us. We are no longer signposts that point the way. In Jesus we have become the road map!

Our mistake is often to attach our frustration to anywhere else except our own relationship with the Lord. This is a *paidion* activity. It is adolescent spirituality. It reveals our own immaturity. We are not preparing the way of the Lord; we are condemning the church for not moving with God.

If we are too long in negative emotions without a sense of purpose, they become destructive. We can be frustrated because we feel strongly that something should be happening now! It is important here to know the difference between timing and time. Our frustration tells us that it is time. We have entered the place where something should be happening. Now we need to know the Lord's specific timing and how to prepare ourselves for an event in the Spirit. Timing belongs to God, preparation belongs to us!

Now we need to be the agents of change. We must speak to what is coming and prepare the way of the Lord. To do that effectively we must examine our own heart, motives, and method of delivery.

Change will be resisted by the enemy. If the heart of the one prophesying is not in the right place with God, the enemy can and will use our words to slow down any movement and create inertia. Our frustration becomes a self-fulfilling prophecy. We have been blindsided by the devil and our message has been subverted.

We can have the right message but deliver it so poorly that it is rejected not because of its content, but because the transmission was faulty. There has to be a change in us first, so that we can authenticate the message through our delivery.

Frustration is a sign that something needs to change in us but that we have not yet recognized or acknowledged it. What are we currently not seeing? What if there is more than God wants to show us but our negativity means He cannot trust us with further revelation? It is true that we do see through a glass darkly. What if the Father wants to clean up our perspective so that we see more clearly?

Prophecy must pass on the heart of God to the people around. Our frustration is a clue to what is our own relational adjustment. This is a hard lesson for most *paidions* to grasp. Failure here means that we remain relationally and prophetically adolescent.

Frustration may also be a sign that we are carrying some prejudice against a person, a group, or a particular vision. God allows us our preferences but not our prejudice! Always ask the questions: "What is this frustration for? What do you want to show me? What must change in me so that I can be a catalyst for change?" If I change, I can bring change!

Frustration is God opening a door of opportunity to an individual, a group, or a church. He wants us to put our foot in the door whilst He changes our heart and perception. Frustration can signal the end of one thing and the start of something new. If something new is forming we must discern what needs to be retained and how it fits with the new thing that is happening. In order to see what the new anointing might be, we first must go to a deeper level of relationship with the Lord. We need to take responsibility for what our frustration means in our personal walk with the Lord.

Our frustration is a clue to our own adjustment

All our frustrations are primarily tied into our relationship with God first, and our gifting and function second. *Paidions* do the opposite of this mostly.

Often when I am with other churches and I sense a high degree of frustration, I have to help them make sense of it for themselves personally and corporately. It is important that I allow the Lord to use my heart effectively to be a catalyst for faith and hope to rise.

This is vital. People tell prophets what is not happening. They will share their frustrations, irritations, and exasperations. Do not fire someone else's bullets! We are there to develop the priorities of a proper response to the Lord. We must change our own internal environment so that we take on the nature of God in that context. This is where wisdom is more powerful and profound than prophetic revelation.

Wisdom knows how God thinks, how He perceives the situation, what He plans to do about it, and how He wants to do it. David said, "*Make me to know your ways Lord, teach me your paths. Lead me in your truth and teach me."* (Psalm 25:4–5)

Prophets always ask the reason for the frustration. What if there is no progress because something else needs to happen that has a higher priority with the Lord? For example, what if we are holding onto our carnality in this situation rather than taking it to the cross? A major part of teaching and discipling people is to enable them to take hold of themselves in order to see the priority in the purposes of God. There is no doubt that the fruit of self-control enables us to see in the Spirit what our negative emotions are shielding through our prejudice.

God allows us our preferences, but not our prejudice

Frustration creates tension. If a prophet is frustrated he cannot release, only bind. There is no movement without tension. If I want to lift a cup I must tense my fingers so that I can get a grip properly. Tension does not mean that there is something wrong. It means that something is happening. We must ensure that our tension does not become a friction, and for that we need the oil of the Holy Spirit. All moving parts need lubrication or they seize up.

The whole point of frustration therefore to a prophet is to highlight where he needs to partner with the Holy Spirit so that fresh oil can be poured out.

The Difference Between False and Poor Prophecy

Anyone can fall into false prophecy, but *paidions* are especially at risk of being poor prophets. There is a big difference between *poor* and *false* prophecy.

False prophecy is deceptive and deliberately leads people away from the Lord. Often it is a word dreamt up in human imagination and thoughts (Jeremiah 23:16–18). People speak out of the deception of their own hearts (Jeremiah 23:26). Deception is a lifestyle issue. It does not arrive overnight and is usually caused by a lack of real accountability. Such people should be treated cautiously, especially those ministries that are not rooted in a local church.

False prophecy comes out of people's own inspirations — they have seen nothing and are simply inventing words (Ezekiel 13:1–3). People prophesy from their own human souls for their own devious ends. Today, as in times of Scripture, we have people prophesying for money (Micah 3:11). Peter warned the New Testament church about false, money-hungry prophets in 2 Peter 2:3: *"And in their greed they will exploit you with false words."*

Often, false prophecy speaks exactly what others want to hear. It is an effort by manipulative people to curry favour and gain control over other people's lives or to bind people into churches or churches into networks.

We can never dismiss a false prophecy as insignificant. The enemy uses words, too, and false prophecy should be treated like a curse. It opens the door to sinister human and demonic activity. These people need to be rooted out and dealt with justly. The church must cut down the territory in which these people operate.

Poor prophecy, however, often occurs because of inexperience and poor practice that has gone unchecked and uncorrected. This type of prophecy is impure because it mixes too much of our own thoughts with the words the Lord has given, leading to distortion.

In the early days of the charismatic movement, people were often in revolt against form and tradition. For a while, the pendulum swung away from those things as people delighted in spontaneity and being led by the Spirit in all things. Inevitably, it became crass and hyper-spiritual. Some people eschewed leaders, preferring to be wholly led by the Spirit. Others indulged in meetings where very little happened because everyone was waiting for the Lord to tell them what to do. Occasionally, things worked out wonderfully well and the meeting was touched by God. Mostly, the people who had the loudest voices or were the most outspoken took over the meeting and "ministered" to the others. Planning and preparation were frowned upon as unspiritual or lacking in faith. All of this "enforced spontaneity" had an impact on the prophetic. A number of misunderstandings grew up around prophecy, many of which have persisted over the decades to the present day.

Ignorance is not ungodly

First, there was the *golden rule of spontaneity* that we did not have to prepare anything — simply "open our mouths and God would give us the words." This fallacy about prophecy was built on various Scriptures, including Matthew 10:19–20, Mark 13:11, Luke 12:11–12, Luke 21:12–15, Exodus 4:12, and 2 Peter 1:21.

However, as we shall see by looking at a few of those passages, the Bible is talking about a word of testimony, not a word of prophecy. The context is that when preaching the gospel, we could be dragged before important people who will demand explanations for our message. "*When they arrest you and hand you over, do not worry beforehand about what you are to say, but say whatever is given you in that hour; for it is not you who speak, but it is the Holy Spirit,*" says Mark 13:11. This clearly refers to testimony, not prophecy, as does Luke 21:12–15: "*But before all these things, they will lay their hands on you and will persecute you, delivering you to the synagogues and prisons, bringing you before kings and governors for My name's sake. It will lead to an opportunity for your testimony. So make up your minds not to prepare beforehand to defend yourselves; for I will give you utterance and wisdom which none of your opponents will be able to resist or refute.*"

Jesus is instructing His disciples about the kind of attitudes they must adopt when called to explain the gospel. First, do not worry. Second, do not premeditate your answers. Third, use it as a time to give your testimony. It has nothing to do with prophecy. Jesus' principles were used by Peter and John in Acts 4 when they were called to face Annas, Caiaphas, and the rulers of the law.

The Old Testament passage refers to Moses, who had been given a charge to go to Egypt and command Pharaoh to "let my people go" on behalf of the Lord. Moses protested because he was slow of speech and clearly believed he would embarrass both God and himself. God's reply in Exodus 4:12 was blunt: "*Now then go, and I, even I, will be with your mouth, and teach you what you are to say.*"

This order had nothing to do with prophecy. Moses had to give a command from Almighty God to the world's most powerful ruler. In those circumstances, we would all be apprehensive. However, Moses' sense of inadequacy was so strong that he could not trust God to help him. The Lord eventually gave him Aaron as a mouthpiece.

People are often fond of quoting 2 Peter 1:21: "*For no prophecy was ever made by an act of human will, but men moved by the Holy Spirit spoke from God.*" Again, we must examine the context into which the word was spoken. The Bible is referring to the prophecy of Scripture, not the gift of prophecy and spontaneous prophetic utterance. Scripture did not come out of human creativity and inspiration. To be certain, God used the talents, education, and cultural backgrounds of each writer, but Scripture itself is God-breathed and given by His inspiration. (2 Timothy 3:16)

Spontaneity by itself is seldom purposeful

When we apply these Scriptures to spontaneously moving in the gift of prophecy, we take them out of their original context. When we take Scripture out of context, we make it a pretext to do things that are unbiblical.

I do not believe that all prophecy must be meticulously prepared and well-rehearsed before it is delivered. I do believe, however, that to move in prophecy effectively, we need a solid understanding of Scripture, the character of God, and the nature of His ways. Without that essential foundation, we are vulnerable in our ignorance and we may speak out of the well of what we do not know.

Prophecy is a mix of the Holy Spirit drawing upon our knowledge and experiences of God, our understanding of Scripture, our times of prayer, communion, preparation, and spontaneous utterance. These elements, I believe, are a prerequisite for moving in prophecy, and we cannot rely upon the mood of the moment.

There are times when certain prophetic words are prepared, rehearsed, and planned. They are words of weight and importance, carrying great significance. At other times, we receive the bones of a prophecy with key words and phrases that are fleshed out as we speak. Then there are times when we receive certain impressions that need to be followed up carefully and with wisdom. Over the years, I have given hundreds of spontaneous prophetic words. However, the course of my life is set upon the road of prayer, meditation, study of Scripture, and communion with the Lord.

To move out in prophecy without that sure foundation is to produce weak prophecy that will be impure and distorted and lead to error. It is a *paidion* form of revelation.

Another common mistake is that physical sensations are the indicator of the presence of the Holy Spirit. Our hearts begin to beat rapidly, the hair on our neck stands up, our palms are sweaty, and we have a sense that something is brewing. These feelings could be rooted in several things.

First, it may simply be nerves. Many people get very nervous at the mere thought that God may want us to do something, even before we have discerned what it is. He may want us to pray or read out a Scripture; it does not always mean we should move out in the prophetic.

Second, the Holy Spirit may just want to speak to us personally. What we hear is private and not for general distribution at that point. We must always be careful to share any revelation with mature people to avoid deception and increase understanding.

Third, the Holy Spirit is brooding over us. The attendant physical feelings may be His way of getting our attention. On many occasions, I have not delivered any word, prophetic or otherwise, at that point. The Holy Spirit has indicated that He wishes to speak and wants me to draw aside and listen. It may signify that a time of prayer, fasting, or preparation is required.

Some prophecy can wait a day or more, depending on what the Holy Spirit is doing. I held one word for more than two years while praying for the right person to emerge to give it to. Sometimes the beginning of a word needs a time of preparation and prayer in order for it to mature before delivery. We may need to come aside and seek God specifically.

Many times I have seen so-called prophecies fall flat because people could not discern what was happening at the time. They had a couple of words and moved out prophetically, only to discover there was no more and that they would need to fill out the word with their own perceptions in order to cover their mistake.

This is an immature, adolescent, *paidion* form of prophecy. We must allow God to mature and test us so we can move into becoming full-fledged sons and daughters of the Most High.

It is important as leaders that we know the difference between discipline and punishment. We discipline people so that they can receive more of the Holy Spirit and so that they can have space to grow up safely in the Lord. Everyone needs to be discipled and developed so that their progress is evident to the whole church. We must make every situation as positive a learning experience as possible.

> ***Discipline without development is punishment***

Discipline without development is punishment. To prevent someone speaking prophetically but not to provide training and loving feedback is the antithesis of God's nature. There is nothing finer than loving correction given by someone who believes in us and wants to see us develop.

The moment we have to stop people from doing things in leadership or ministry is the prime moment of reflection where we must turn the light on ourselves regarding accountability. What is our attitude towards this person?

Is there a relational breakdown between us? What do I find difficult to trust in them or their gifting and how do I partner with the Spirit to adjust that effectively? Are they operating out of a present–past lifestyle where woundedness is dominating how they speak? How do I bring healing and wholeness? Are they just too much hassle for me at this time? Do I have the love and grace necessary to enable them to breakthrough? What faith and patience do I need in this relationship?

Of course there are many more questions that we can ask, depending on the people involved and the particular circumstances. The point I am making is that we get extraordinary opportunities at inconvenient moments. The prime role of leadership is the development of the body of Christ and the building of the house of the Lord. We must grow people in the spirit before we build them into the work.

The elements of poor prophecy usually involve the following:

- People venting their own frustration
- Forcing their own thoughts on others
- Speaking out their pet theory
- Relating what they want to happen
- Speaking out of their ruling passion
- Speaking out of untested revelation because of a general ignorance of Scripture
- Firing other peoples' bullets unintentionally

These are to name but a few. Mostly it can come under the heading of soulish opinions dressed up as prophecy and with a "thus says the Lord" attached in an attempt to give the word some weight.

James had some good insights into this type of situation. In James 3:17–18 we read: *"But the wisdom from above is first pure, then peaceable, gentle, reasonable, full of mercy and good fruits, unwavering, without hypocrisy. And the seed whose fruit is righteousness is sown in peace by those who make peace."*

The word from above is *pure*. It has no mixture and the motive behind it is clean. It is *peaceable* because it is delivered in a way that is compatible with the language of heaven and the Prince of Peace. It is *gentle* and easy to receive. Even if the word has some hard things being communicated, it is not harshly spoken. It is *willing to yield*, which means it can be challenged. It is open to correction. People who know that prophecy must be evaluated are often more open in their communication of it.

Prophecy is *full of mercy* because it acts in line with the gospel of grace. It is the goodness and the kindness of God that leads us to repentance. A prophecy must be good news, even if that news is repent! It is *full of good fruits*. The attitude of the one speaking is good and wholesome. Their words are challenging but revealing of God's nature. It ministers grace to the hearers. It edifies, exhorts, and brings comfort.

It is *without partiality* and does not take any sides. It fires no bullets. It is not opinionated or prejudiced in any way. It is thoroughly impartial and only seeks to represent God's will. Finally, it is *without hypocrisy*. It is teachable. It has no double standards. People cannot prophesy to bring repentance when they have issues they are not addressing in their own lives.

"The fruit of righteousness is sown in peace by those who make peace." We are always sowing into the nature of God. We are partakers of the divine nature (2 Peter 1:4). The effect of prophecy is edification, encouragement, and the blessing of God's comforting presence when we need Him most.

Prophets release a word so that people can turn or return to God. At times a prophecy may have to necessarily cut across a particular meeting in order to release something that the Lord may want to do in that particular gathering.

Both prophets and leaders must practice James 3:17–18 in regard to prophecy. If both groups commit themselves to this process we will develop understanding and trust within the work, and the Lord will continue to speak. Our goal here is that the church becomes a prophetic people and a prophetic voice into our culture. We are not just concerned with having a few people moving in the gift of prophecy. We want to become a prophetic community where the word of the Lord is a normal part of our lives and relationships.

The church is a prophetic community in words and actions

If we do not practice the above we may become a breeding ground for suspicion and mistrust. Then we will become hard of hearing. And the Lord will not speak because He does not trust the prophet's mouth or the church's ears!

Adopted as Huios

The first three stages of Christian maturity — *nepios, teknon,* and *paidion* — are steps in a journey towards our ultimate goal, being a *huios* son or daughter. *Huios* is a grown-up child who can be trusted fully by their parents.

In biblical times, a ceremony took place when a son had grown up enough to be trusted by his father. Throughout his childhood, the boy would be given various tasks to accomplish and tests to be passed. He had to prove his ability to cope with certain situations. When he failed a test, he was given it again and again until he passed it. Some tests were deliberately unfair and skewed. This wasn't cruelty on the father's part; instead, it was an opportunity for a son to prove his truthfulness, faithfulness, integrity, and godliness.

When a son had proved himself, the father would call an adoption ceremony. He would invite all of his neighbors and present the young man to them. "This is my son, in whom I am well-pleased," the dad would say aloud. The implications of that statement were massive. From that moment on, the son's word was guaranteed by the father. When the son signed a check, it was as if the father had signed it. When the younger man entered a contract, it was as if the older one had. They were one and the same. One's word was the other's. The young man had moved into the status of being a *huios.*

To be a son of God we must pass our tests

Obviously, this understanding of adoption is very different from how our culture uses the word. Today, an adoption occurs when we take a child who is not our own and treat them as though they are ours. Over the years, some people have taught that we are the devil's children, bound by sin, and then adopted by God into His family. This is bad theology and incorrect teaching. When we are born again, God is our Father. His divine nature is within us. If it were possible to be adopted by God as we use the term today, we wouldn't need to be born again. God wants natural children, not legal ones.

The ceremony of adoption and the recognition of *huios* maturity had everything to do with the promotion of a son or daughter found to be trustworthy. "*For all who are being led by the Spirit of God, these are sons of God,*" Paul wrote in Romans 8:14. "Sons" in that verse is the Greek word *huios.* The first three stages of our maturity are child stages; *huios* is about being a full-fledged son or daughter. We are all children of God, but we are not all yet sons of God. "*For you have not received a spirit of slavery leading to fear again, but you received a spirit of adoption by which we cry out, 'Abba, Father,'* " Paul continued in verse 15. *Abba* and *pater,* the Greek form of "father," are very distinctive words and reinforce the progression of maturity. *Abba* is the same as a young child saying "Daddy." *Pater* is the term for father that fully matured children use. People who need an *abba* need help; people who use the word *pater* are offering to help any way they can. The transition from *abba* to *pater* is another part of the adoption ceremony.

When God deems a Christian to be ready to move from *paidion* to *huios,* a ceremony of adoption takes place in the Spirit. All of the sudden, heaven seems to fall on the individual. They just take off in the things of God. We often associate that with ministry but it really has very little to do with that aspect. Instead, it is all about coming to the place where God can trust us. When God trusts a person, nothing can stop them. At Jesus' baptism, the Holy Spirit descended on Him in the form of a dove, and a voice from Heaven adopted Him. After thirty years of obedience and hiddenness, the Father trusted the Son fully. He received an anointing He had never walked in before. Being a *huios* son or daughter means there is a consistency present in our lives. We have learned how to wait on God and tend to His agenda for our lives.

In Luke 6:35, Jesus outlined four things a *huios* needs to do: *"But love your enemies, and do good, and lend, expecting nothing in return; and your reward will be great, and you will be sons of the Most High."* These four things have a common bond: they require living outside ourselves. We stop doing everything to get something; instead, we live to serve God and others. We do things because they are right. The immature do things to be recognized or honored, but the mature do what they have to do for God's glory. They sow because it is the right thing to do.

God lifts His *huios* sons and daughters to new levels of thinking and being. He gives us a taste of what is to come and allows us to see things from a different level.

Everything in our lives exists to test us in our journey toward being a trusted son or daughter of God. At first, we are tested in the small things. Do we show up on time? Are we willing to submit our revelation to the proper channels? Are we willing to help set up chairs or tidy the church kitchen? *Huios* has nothing to do with age or years as a Christian, but is a measure of our inner man. In life, maturity comes through experience, wisdom, and knowledge. In the spiritual realm, it comes from God's dealings with us on a spiritual level, and how obedient, faithful, and responsive to discipline we are.

> *Children have not developed consistency*

God is not satisfied with children — He wants fully grown sons and daughters. We all have to accept God's discipline in order to partake in His holiness. When we get into the practice of responding to the slightest touch of the Holy Spirit, we give Him what He wants. In the early stages, this discipline seems onerous, but our lives are not our own anyway. We belong to God, and part of maturing in Him is to check everything in our hearts, minds, mouths, and spirits.

We react to this personal discipline in four different ways. *Nepios* babies get angry and run away as fast as their little legs will carry them. *Teknon* children misunderstand God's motives in the discipline. They often think such discipline is the enemy trying to oppress them. They blame everything on everyone else or on the devil. *Paidion* teenagers accept the need for discipline but fall into self-pity when it occurs. But *huios* adults know how to kiss the hand that hurts them. They accept God's discipline gratefully and submit to His control. "Change me," a *huios* says.

Handling Wrong Prophecy

Because of this humble, trustworthy attitude, a *huios* is the person who needs to handle wrong prophecy in a church. *"Brethren, even if anyone is caught in any trespass, you who are spiritual, restore such a one in a spirit of gentleness; each one looking to yourself, so that you too will not be tempted,"* Paul wrote in

Galatians 6:1. Restoration, meekness, and consideration for others are all vital elements in the redemptive process.

In Matthew 18:15, Jesus counseled us to win over our brothers who are in the wrong. We can't just drop people; such actions are ungodly. Instead, we have to search for the sheep who has gone astray and bring it home rejoicing. Be honest in loving confrontation. Admit your own faults if you contributed to the situation in any way. Feedback is a vital skill that all leaders must develop and use. Some will excel more than others. If we are to disciple, train, equip, and release people into their giftings, we must recognize that effective constructive criticism is essential.

It is a completely natural and normal way of life to evaluate events, business deals, sporting performances, films, meals, friendships, learning experiences, and other things. All of us have been evaluated many times over. Sometimes, we are completely unaware that we are being appraised. At other times, we can find the experience painful and occasionally humiliating. Rarely, it seems, do we enjoy the experience. That can be due in part to the assessor's lack of expertise, our own defensiveness, or simply the fact that the learning curve we were on at the time was too great and thus produced a lot of mistakes. No one is born with the ability to analyze and review the actions of others. It is a skill that must be learned. Sadly, it is an aptitude that is never taught in church, even though it is a vital part of discipleship and training.

We must regain the lost art of loving feedback

When evaluating people who move in the gift of prophecy, we must first examine their attitudes. A humble, servant spirit is required to bring the word of the Lord. The word may be spoken boldly and with power. People may be strong and forceful in their deliveries, and yet the underlying spirit is one of meekness and tenderness of heart. Moses was a prophet often speaking with a great courage, yet he was the meekest man on earth. Meekness is not weakness, but strength under control. How people conduct themselves before, during, and after they have prophesied all deserve observation and comment. We can have the right word but deliver it in the wrong spirit, thus negating what we say because people cannot receive our attitudes.

The method of delivery is the second thing to look for in people. Presentation is very important. Was it overbearing or pompous? Did they speak too long? Did they rush their words? Were they ill-at-ease or confident? Were the words clearly spoken? Did they make sense? Did the prophecy flow with the meeting or cut across it? Either of these last two points can be right. I have seen meetings rescued from obscurity by a prophetic word. Were they creative in their presentation? At times, we can use music, drama, or props to symbolize what God is saying. Assessing the methods of delivery and perhaps making appropriate suggestions will cause people to consider important points other than the context of the word.

Handling Wrong Prophecy

Third, was the word screened properly? Some words need to be filtered through the leadership beforehand; was it one of these? When examining a prophecy, it is helpful for leaders to have someone present who is strongly prophetic. The person who is giving the word (however inexperienced) should occasionally sit in on these times. It will aid their growth and development.

Fourth, however poor the performance, always ensure that the assessment is as positive as possible. We must be truthful, but we can also be gracious. Do not forget to express thanks to people who put themselves out on a limb in this way. Make suitable recommendations and give necessary advice. Where it is appropriate, we can outline specific boundaries for the gift in the immediate future. People should prophesy according to the proportion of their faith (Romans 12:6). We can tell by experience when someone has gone beyond their measure or, alternatively, has not lived up to it. Sometimes we need to put restraints on people's gifts to allow their characters to catch up. At other times, they need to stay at a particular level to fully develop their confidence and experience.

Finally, we can enlist their help in administering the prophecy. We can ask them for suggestions in terms of the next step on how we are to proceed. These suggestions may not be helpful, but it is still a useful process to go through.

Over a period of time, our evaluations will help us to determine a pattern of strengths and weaknesses for each individual. These elements can be worked out during the discipleship process. Once people get used to friendly, helpful, and realistic feedback, the process will become easier to administrate.

Handling Wrong Prophecy in a Meeting

In our meetings, we need to strike the right balance between encouraging the gift of prophecy and guarding the flock from potentially damaging words. We also need to protect the meeting from being hijacked by unstable people.

Most churches opt for a process of correction or prevention. Those who are involved in the correction of incidents normally operate that way because they *a)* believe that everyone has the right to speak and no one should be denied the opportunity, and/or *b)* have not thought through the implications of letting the prophetic loose in the church without adequate supervision and support.

Every ministry requires proper definition and sufficient restraint to maintain a satisfactory balance. Having one without the other is like a bird with one wing — it can only go around in circles. Problems will, likewise, keep coming around. There are only so many responses we can make from the platform when wrong prophecy has occurred.

One option is to draw no attention to the event at the time. It may just be best to keep the meeting flowing rather than make any observations following a bad word. We do need to follow up on the situation with a quiet word after the meeting. However, it may not be worth taking action during the session;

it may be a matter of saying, "Well, moving on!" It is as good a time as any to make announcements or conduct the offering, and move on.

Second, if the situation warrants it, we may have to make some kind of comment or observation. We do not want to demolish people or have a public confrontation — we want to act maturely and responsibly. Try to say something bland, if possible: "Thank you for those thoughts. We appreciate people sharing what they feel." We are not calling it prophecy, and we are not getting behind it. We are just bridging the gap between their words and the rest of the meeting. Naturally, our responses will depend upon what has been said and the manner in which it came forth. Try to respond without any heat or edge in your voice. Keep a calm, measured, and mild tone. "I believe that was our brother/sister's own spirit speaking; let's move on."

Accountability is about finding our freedom

At other times, people may go right over the top, leaving us no alternative but to give a public rebuke. We are gathered for a purpose; therefore, we do not want this situation to become a focal point. Our aim is to neutralize what was said, caution the individual, avoid confusion in the congregation, and improve the tone of the meeting.

Again, let me emphasize that we can do all of this without unnecessary heat. There is no need for us to make this situation worse by provoking a conflict. If a soft answer turns away wrath (Proverbs 15:1), then a rebuke without heat will defuse a potentially explosive situation. We do not have to prove our authority at times like this. We just have to act like our loving Father, as a *huios* son or daughter should. Where necessary, we can give a short, reasoned explanation.

There are three situations in which we should publicly rebuke people for poor prophecy:

1. If they have given a directional word or a judgmental word, we need to let them know the following: "That type of prophecy is out of order in a public setting. The place for directional/correctional words is in the leadership, so that they can be judged and weighed in the appropriate manner. I suggest we pray together and get on with what the Lord is doing." That takes about fifteen seconds to say and allows us to move on. We will probably need to reinforce the right protocol in prophecy from time to time.

2. If a harsh or condemning word has been spoken, our response can be: "I do not witness to that word. It is not the voice of the Lord. Let's just concentrate on the Lord Jesus right now. We do not want anything to interfere with our worship or the moving of the Holy Spirit." We can then go into a song, prayer, or another activity.

3. If a person has prophesied their own opinion or shown a bad attitude, our response could be: "Brother/sister, I believe that is your own opinion. You are speaking out of your own frustration. Meetings are not the place for that. I would be happy to chat with you later." Then we can move on.

Be mild, kind, speak softly, and smile. Be quietly emphatic and only take a few seconds to reply. Take the sting out of the situation and then press on. Give a mild reproof, then let your voice pick up a gear as you focus people's attention on the next thing. Don't give utterances the title of prophecy. Call it a word; it is less demeaning to the prophetic.

Some churches operate in prevention mode. They guard the flock very defensively. It can be almost impossible to prophesy from the body of the congregation and they would frown on such freedom anyway. I have often found that such "covering" is based on distrust. They lay a minefield designed almost to protect the church from prophecy.

Picture the scene: we believe we have a prophecy. To make ourselves heard, we have to go to the front of the meeting and use a microphone. On the way there, we encounter the platform policeman. This is the person who guards the microphone from the attack of people with the spirit of splutter! We now have to convince him that God is really speaking to us. This is almost impossible to convey in a few brief sentences. In full view of the congregation, we try to put our thoughts into a credible pattern. The platform policeman has only a matter of minutes to discern the voice of the Lord. Imagine the embarrassment when the policeman says no, and we have to slink back to our seat. Everyone has seen our rejection.

Does this scene seem all too familiar to many of us? How many of us have had any loving follow-up that explained why we were not permitted to speak?

To be fair, it is very difficult for both sides to express themselves in those situations. Often the music is blaring out of a loudspeaker just a few steps away while the congregation is engaged in noisy worship. The policeman role sometimes exists because we have never taught the whole church about prophecy. We have not created prophetic climates or environments where the church knows that only mature and gifted people can speak prophetically from the front. It is a climate where people don't know about inspirational and revelational prophecies.

If we want our people to grow in the prophetic in public gatherings, the least we can do is put mature, prophetic people on duty at the back of the hall rather than in full public view. If our platform policemen are there to discourage people from reaching the microphone, we have completely missed the point of body ministry and effective training and development. We must not make people run the gauntlet; it is unfair and humiliating!

At the back of the meeting, it is often more quiet and peaceful. The mature person can listen attentively to the individual and the Lord. An explanation can be given quietly and lovingly if we consider it unwise to proceed with the word. The potential giver can be thanked and blessed without feeling stupid. No one else will see what is happening. Alternatively, the person with the word can be escorted to the platform by the mature prophet, giving a sign of approval to the church rather than the current disapproval that most people experience.

Growing Into Huios Sons and Daughters

The way to transition into maturity is to accept and embrace accountability. When we do that, we grow from being Jacob the schemer into Israel, the prince of the people of God. People often fear accountability because of previous negative experiences. But true accountability is one of the most freeing moments of a Christian's life.

Accountability is a journey from being controlled by others to being self-controlled. Control is a fact of life; either we control ourselves or someone controls us. If we all policed ourselves, we wouldn't need a police force. But some people are unable to exercise self-control; therefore, they need to be controlled by other authority figures. A child, for example, cannot control himself, so a parent or teacher must teach him that discipline. Leaders in churches are not there to govern people. They are there to bring other Christians to a place where they can govern their own lives.

To be a *huios* son or daughter, God must break our capacity for self-rule. The true message of the cross is "not My will, but Yours be done." We must emulate Christ in that spirit. If we have to be governed by our leadership, there is something wrong with us. We are behaving like children, not grown sons and daughters.

We must love to learn the ways of God. The truth does indeed set us free, but before it does, it bothers us. When we are trying to assimilate truth into our own lives, it's like a burr under a saddle. Something is not right and it grates on us. But this process is vital for us to develop the will to be transformed into someone more like Jesus. If we love the truth, we will walk in it no matter the cost. When Pilate asked Jesus if He was a king, the Lord's reply was clear: "*You say correctly that I am a king. For this I have been born, and for this I have come into the world, to testify to the truth. Everyone who is of the truth hears My voice*" (John 18:37). Jesus was all about the truth.

Accountability isn't about coming under someone. It is about being willing to submit ourselves to the will of God. Accountability helps us realize our potential. We see ourselves as Christ does and can respond to that vision. In an effort to be more like Him, we embrace accountability as an aid to developing a personality free from sin.

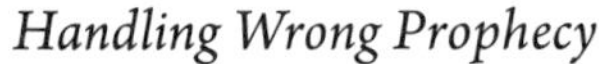

It should be easy for people to speak the truth in love to us. I have often found that the more defensive we are, the less we love the truth. In accountability, our attitude should be simple: "I trust God." To trust the people around us more, we must trust the Father fully. We cannot release horizontal faith in people until we have worked out our vertical faith in God. The moment we truly believe who God is, we can trust people.

God operates relationally. He cannot do otherwise, because to deny that He is love goes against every fiber of His being. We have to trust in Him and that His promises to us — such as God causes all things to work together for good to those who love Him, to those who are called according to His purpose — are true. When we believe in Him fully, we can trust that He is behind everything that is happening in our lives.

It is very difficult to notice our own blind spots. Fortunately, accountability helps reveal them to us. We should have people in our lives that we trust more than ourselves. In my life, there are people who I trust to show me where I am falling down, becoming apathetic, or not meeting the potential God has put in me.

This kind of accountability is very difficult for some people but I believe that the issue is about our faith in God, not humanity. To me, it's a win-win. If someone brings an issue to my attention and he is right, I can change it and become something more than I am. On the flip side, if I am wrongly accused of something and I accept that accountability, I lose my pride. That humility still strengthens me spiritually. I have nothing to lose in the process. Being accountable is not about being crucified by someone. In fact, we are already dead because of what Christ has done for us. It is about seeing the potential to be something more.

Accountability doesn't just change us, it transforms us. Change comes out of transformation, but transformation is not birthed by change. In friendship, we must be working to transform people into more of who Jesus has made them to be.

This distinction is more than just semantics. Transformation is an internal realignment which occurs in our inner being and is birthed by the Holy Spirit. Change, on the other hand, is an external adjustment. True change is the fruit of transformation.

It is very possible to be touched by God but not changed. Samson, for example, was incredibly anointed by God but his character was a disaster. This man of God who was raised up to be a champion in the nation became a prisoner of the very people he was called to overcome. He ended up bald, blind, and bound in the temple of his enemy. He was a laughingstock; the only way to redeem his call was to pull down the entire building and kill himself. Was that the plan of God

> *We can be touched by God but not changed*

for Samson? No way! In the end, Samson was a victim of his own soulish nature. He refused accountability and never achieved the full purposes of God.

Similarly, Solomon had a tremendous relationship with God at the beginning. He asked for wisdom and was given every blessing God had. What a sight it must have been the day Solomon's temple was dedicated! The presence of God was so thick that no one could stand up. And yet this mighty king ended his life broken, bitter, and devoured by his own lust. He had never been transformed by God.

His father, David, however, welcomed accountability. After stealing a man's wife and conspiring to murder him, Nathan the prophet came to David. Nathan told a story of a rich man who had stolen a poor man's beloved lamb. The story cut David to the core. When he realized that he was that thief, he immediately repented and turned to God. That day transformed and changed him.

Nathan had been successful because he had spoken out of a well of love. The truth he presented David devastated the king but, ultimately, set him free. His accountability had transformed him. Despite his crimes, David found the grace of God and lived on as a *huios* son. That is true accountable and mature behavior: humble, penitent, and reliant on God for everything.

Accountability is about freedom. "*It is for freedom that Christ has set us free*" (Galatians 5:1). There is no freedom without responsibility. We must understand who we are now and who we are becoming under the hand of God.

Accountability is about process — the series of steps from where I am now to where the Lord wants me to be in Him. This is what we mean by walking with the Lord and working out our salvation with Him. We are totally engaged in the process of becoming more of who we are in Christ. It's the process that makes us rich, not the outcome. Accountability is about self-knowledge perfected. It means that we know two things about ourselves: (a) what we are like without Christ, and (b) who we are in Christ now and who we are becoming in Him as we journey with the Holy Spirit.

Accountability is about assuming ownership and responsibility for the journey, the process of God. It is the power to walk with God through your own transformation and to enjoy the journey.

Notes

Notes

Notes

Handling Wrong Prophecy

Reflections, Exercises and Assignments

The following exercises are designed with this particular chapter in mind. Please work through them carefully before going on to the next chapter. Take time to reflect on your life journey as well as your prophetic development. Learn to work well with the Holy Spirit and people that God has put around you so that you will grow in grace, humility, and wisdom in the ways of God.

Graham Cooke.

What Constitutes Maturity?

There is no maturity without adequate self-knowledge. We must know what we are like without Jesus operating fully in our lives. We must also be aware of where we are at any moment in time regarding who we are in Jesus now and who we are becoming.

Maturity is about opening ourselves up to the insights, prayers, and advice of other people. To grow continuously we must love the learning that all situations present to us.

We must grow through our mistakes and develop relationships of worth and value that can empower us to do the right thing. Maturity is learning the ways of God and cultivating a heart and an attitude that is not resistant to change.

Within the context of this chapter, you must be willing and able to develop these attributes as a sign of your growing maturity.

- You should be able to know, understand, and walk in each of the different stages of relationship with the Lord. It's important to know what you are currently learning about yourself and the Lord and where the key place of your commitment is in growing up in Christ. You should be able to ask for help in specific areas of your development.
- It is one battle to get free and another battle to stay free. The enemy always contests the ground of our newfound freedom. The Lord allows that in order to establish the victory in breakthrough as a part of our new freedom in lifestyle. Maturity is in complying with that strategy in order to enhance your freedom. It means often turning our insecurity into a joyful vulnerability in the Lord.
- Developing a relationship with the Holy Spirit is an absolute necessity. In Him we learn to overturn our childish behavior in favor of becoming childlike in Christ.
- Maturity means we are able to conquer ourselves. Understanding the meaning and the purpose of frustration is essential to growth in the Spirit. Learning how to turn negatives into positives so that we are a catalyst for change is vital to our ministry and calling. Mature people see the opportunity in the crisis and learn how to take advantage of them.
- Prophetic maturity knows the difference between false and poor prophecy. Mature people care about standards. They are concerned with excellence. They understand the elements of poor prophecy and are fixed on providing words that truly represent the heart of the Father. They are growing in trust with God and by Him.
- People who want to mature in their prophetic gift are learning all the time. They do not rely on one methodology but practice their gifting

continuously. We can only be truly spontaneous when we have an alternative. Mature people develop the art of crafting prophecy in relationship with the Holy Spirit.

- Non-accountable people soon reach the place where trusting them becomes difficult. Mature people take responsibility for their own growth. They love the freedom of honest, open relationships. They are not afraid of truth but relish its presence in their lives. They seek out loving, accountable relationships with people who are experienced in the truth.

What Constitutes Immaturity?

Immature people wait for God to come to them. They do not take responsibility to seek God or to pursue righteousness. They tolerate sin and often have to come under conviction from God before they consider changing. Really immature people attract chastisement because they seldom pay attention to the simple delightful pleasure of continuous adjustment by the Holy Spirit.

Not to love discipline and transformation is to invite chastisement. Immature people usually have to learn the hard way. The cross is not painful unless we resist it. Immaturity is mostly centered on our own selfishness, ignorance, and obstructions to change that we construct around our spirituality.

Always learning but never able to come to knowledge of the truth, we become clouds without rain. We have the appearance of being something without the substance to back it up.

Within the context of this chapter, you must face up to the challenges of ongoing immaturity. Here are some possibilities for your consideration.

- You have stayed at this level of your development for too long because you haven't developed a relationship with the Holy Spirit that facilitates ongoing change on a regular basis. You show more commitment to your victim mindset than you do to becoming more Christlike. You justify your behavior based on how you feel rather than on what is right and true in Christ. You do not take up the challenge to become changed that each situation presents. You have an unconscious habit of resisting personal development.
- Personal breakthroughs are lost because you do not win the battle to stay free and establish your freedom. You take several steps forward, then some steps back. Your behavior is more childish than childlike. When corrected, you sulk. When disciplined, you exhibit self-pity. Your relationship with the Holy Spirit is not characterized by the fruit of His personality in your life. Often you lack the simple basis of love, joy, peace, and patience.

- You have a tendency to be ruled by frustration, impatience, and exasperation. Your first thoughts may be more negative than positive. Your fellowship with others may slip into criticism. It's easier to see the faults rather than the treasure in someone. You are prone to firing other peoples' bullets if you are not already manufacturing missiles yourself! You can focus on negatives and your prophecies are mainly corrective and sometimes harsh. Your view of God is more in line with the Old Testament than the gospel of grace.
- Your prophesying is usually in the moment. Spontaneity rules. Your prayer life has not been upgraded for a while and therefore you find it difficult to practice and prepare prophecy before delivery. Your gifting has not increased or grown for a while and is still largely undeveloped even though you have read many books and have been to many training events.
- You are nomadic in your spiritual journey. You have not put roots down in any church community. You have successfully avoided accountability and you hide behind whatever anointing you may be currently generating. You often do not see the test that you are in, let alone have any chance of passing it! Often you cannot tell the difference between spiritual warfare, the disciplines of growth, the work of the cross, or general adversity in life. You blame the enemy and other people for most tough situations because you cannot discern the hand of God.

ASSIGNMENT ONE

Think of a person around your life at this time who is going through a season of difficulty because of opposition, both human and demonic.

Read and meditate on Psalm 124 on that person's behalf. Ask the Lord to touch your heart with His strength and power for that person.

Without quoting the Scripture, put together a prophetic word that will release strength and faith to rise up within them.

To help you craft this prophecy answer the following questions.

1. What is God's objective in this word?

2. What specific encouragements can you release?

3. What are the key words and phrases that come to you as you meditate on this Scripture?

4. What particular promises is God wanting to sow into their situation?

5. What specific opposition will they overcome?

6. What inspiration does God want to impart to them at this time?

7. What can you say that would cause them to see God?

8. How would you say it?

9. Write out the prophetic word on a card and mail it. Alternatively speak the word over them and record it on tape or disc.

ASSIGNMENT TWO

Peace – Fruit of the Spirit

The spiritual fruit of peace is an incredible gift from God. It allows us to get above the hustle and bustle of street-level life and see a bigger picture of what God is doing in and around us. It transports us to a place of rest and absolute confidence in who God wants to be for us. When we realize the omnipotence and power of God, how can we be afraid of any earthly issue?

The power of peace is remarkable. It changes the way we see everything. In 2 Kings 6, Elisha and his servant were surrounded by an army bent on killing both of them. The servant was terrified, but the prophet was completely relaxed.

> *Now when the attendant of the man of God had risen early and gone out, behold, an army with horses and chariots was circling the city. And his servant said to him, "Alas, my master! What shall we do?"*
>
> *So he answered, "Do not fear, for those who are with us are more than those who are with them."*
>
> *Then Elisha prayed and said, "O LORD, I pray, open his eyes that he may see." And the LORD opened the servant's eyes and he saw; and behold, the mountain was full of horses and chariots of fire all around Elisha (2 Kings 6:15–17).*

This story is a perfect example of how peace can pervade any situation. How we feel at any given time is a reflection of our confidence in God. Have we blinded ourselves to His provision and promise? Or are we seeing the host of heaven just a few feet off the ground, ready to strike on our behalf? If there is a situation in your life today causing you anxiety, ask God to come and give you His peace. Ask Him to show you where He is in the situation. What is He wanting to do? The answers to these questions build our peace.

When was a time you felt real, true, godly peace? In your memory bank, go back to that moment. Inhale the peace that resides there. Remember the confidence you had in God at that instant. Now bring that feeling into the present. Look at your life with those same eyes of peace and rest. Stay in the presence of God until you find that peace.

CASE STUDY

Matching prophetic delivery with content

The delivery of a prophetic word must match its content. One cannot shout into a person's face that the Lord is giving them rest and peace. Likewise a prophecy about courage and warrior strength cannot be delivered in a nervous stutter. The context determines what God wants to say and the method of delivery must be in line with God's heart so that the content of the message is fully heard and received as God intended. Study the following prophecy and answer the questions following it.

> *"Julianne, I see a brightly colored parcel, a deep beautiful blue color. It has a huge golden bow wrapped around it. Around the parcel is a silver cord tied to a red balloon. The parcel is floating in mid air.*
>
> *The Lord has already given you many amazing gifts and experiences in the Spirit. There is much, much more that He wants to bestow upon you. There are new gifts, fresh anointings, and brand new experiences that He is releasing to you in these days.*
>
> *His heart is happy for you, over you, and towards you. You are coming completely out of a long season of fighting into a lightness of spirit that will carry you away. This is the year of your rising. This is the year of your rising. You are being called up to occupy a higher place in the Spirit than you could have ever dreamed.*
>
> *To the depths that Satan has ravaged you will be the heights where God shall ravish your heart with love. You shall be the lover of God. There is a new brightness, a new lightness of being that the Lord has gifted you with this new season.*
>
> *This is the time for laughter, not tears — years of joy, a time of dancing, a prolonged season of effortless walking with the Lord your God. He is restoring what the locust has eaten. There are many, many, many creative miracles that the Lord will perform through you, around you, and yes, even to you!*
>
> *Rise up, my beloved, and come away with me. 'For I am laughing,' says the Lord. 'I am rejoicing over you with singing. I delight in you and you shall live a life of delight, untroubled, and restful, even in the midst of battle.'*
>
> *'Come away with Me, my beloved, I am your gift and you are Mine. I shall send you to people and places as My choice gift and everywhere you go, freedom and laughter shall go with you. They will follow you all*

the days of your life and your vengeance on the evil one will be continuous and powerful.' "

1. What is the crux of this word?

2. What is the objective that God has in mind?

3. Notice that the prophecy is unfinished.

   a. What does God want to be for Julianne?

   b. What specific things will the Lord give to Julianne in this situation?

4. What is the outcome that the Lord will guarantee?

5. What is the best way to speak this prophecy?

6. After giving the word, what would you pray over Julianne that would release faith to her?

Handling Wrong Prophecy

LECTIO DIVINA

Lectio Divina (Latin for *divine reading*) is an ancient way of reading the Bible, allowing a quiet and contemplative way of coming to God's Word. *Lectio Divina* opens the pulse of the Scripture, helping readers dig far deeper into the Word than normally happens in a quick glance-over.

In this exercise, we will look at a portion of Scripture and use a modified *Lectio Divina* technique to engage it. This technique can be used on any piece of Scripture; I highly recommend using it for key Bible passages that the Lord has highlighted for you and for anything you think might be an inheritance word for your life (see the *Crafted Prayer* interactive journal for more on inheritance words).

Read the Scripture

> *And He said, "See to it that you are not misled; for many will come in My name, saying, 'I am He,' and, 'The time is near.' Do not go after them. When you hear of wars and disturbances, do not be terrified; for these things must take place first, but the end does not follow immediately."*
>
> *Then He continued by saying to them, "Nation will rise against nation and kingdom against kingdom, and there will be great earthquakes, and in various places plagues and famines; and there will be terrors and great signs from heaven. But before all these things, they will lay their hands on you and will persecute you, delivering you to the synagogues and prisons, bringing you before kings and governors for My name's sake.*
>
> *"It will lead to an opportunity for your testimony. So make up your minds not to prepare beforehand to defend yourselves; I will give you utterance and wisdom which none of your opponents will be able to resist or refute. But you will be betrayed even by parents and brothers and relatives and friends, and they will put some of you to death, and you will be hated by all because of My name.*
>
> *"Yet not a hair of your head will perish. By your endurance you will gain your lives." (Luke 21:8–19)*

1. Find a place of stillness before God. Embrace His peace. Chase the nattering thoughts out of your mind. Calm your body. Breathe slowly. Inhale. Exhale. Inhale. Exhale. Clear yourself of the distractions of life. Whisper the word, "Stillness." Take your time. When you find that rest in the Lord, enjoy it. Worship Him in it. Be with Him there.

2. Reread the passage twice. Allow its words to become familiar to you. Investigate Jesus' prophecy of the end of the age. What images does that bring to your spirit? What do you see? Become a part of it. What phrases or words especially resonate with you? Meditate especially on those shreds of revelation. Write those pieces down in your journal.

3. Read the passage twice again. Like waves crashing onto a shore, let the words of Scripture crash onto your spirit. What excites you? What scares you? What exhilarates you about this revelation of the nature of God? What are you discerning? What are you feeling? What are you hearing? Again, write it all down in your journal.

4. Write the theme of this passage in your journal.

5. Does this passage rekindle any memories or experiences? Does it remind you of any prophetic words you have given or received? Write those down as well.

6. What is the Holy Spirit saying to you through this Scripture? Investigate it with Him — picture the two of you walking through it together. Write those words in your journal.

7. Read the passage two final times. Meditate on it. Is there something God wants you to do? Is there something He is calling you to? Write it down.

8. Pray silently. Tell God what this passage is saying to you. Tell Him what you are thinking about. Write down your conversation together. Picture yourself and the Holy Spirit as two old friends in a coffee shop, chatting about what God is doing.

9. Finally, pray and thank God for His relationship with you. Come back to the passage once a week for the next three months. Read it and let more revelation flow into you. If you feel compelled to, craft a prayer based on this passage for yourself, your family, your friends, or your church. Pray that prayer until you feel God has birthed it in you.

Notes

Notes

Notes

Notes

MODULE FOUR

WORKSHOP & CASE STUDY

Workshop & Case Study

THIS WORKSHOP IS A PERSONAL assignment meant to be undertaken in cooperation with someone from the leadership team of the church who will act as an advisor and assessor. This assignment is in two parts:

1. Choose a family in the church who are not well known to you. Target them for prayer and prophetic encouragement. Follow the process as laid down in this assignment.
2. Write out a Case Study for each step you take. Answer the questions where you see this symbol: CS We want to be able to see your progress throughout the assignment and also the evidence of your accountability and partnership with leaders. Finally, we want to comprehend your thinking and understanding.

THE WORKSHOP

Step One

Choose an individual or a family in your church. Seek the Lord prayerfully (with fasting if required), asking for a word of encouragement for them.

Step Two

Ask the Lord to give you His burden for them at this time. Try to make sure you are receiving His heartbeat for them. Write down what you are sensing as a guideline.

ɕ What is the Lord saying to you through this burden? What are you thinking and feeling?

Step Three

Write down any key words and phrases you receive. Also include pictures, visions, and Scripture you may be sensing.

ɕ Try to determine a pattern to the above (step 3) or an order for them to flow into. Write down the order in this space.

Step Four

What type of word is it?

1. Inspirational and encouraging.
2. Encouragement to overcome a problem.
3. Encouraging and stimulating to faith.
4. Encouraging and challenging.
5. Write down your own preference if different.

This is to enable you to be objective and intentional.

Ꞔ Explain the purpose of your choice above (1–5). It is important to know why you are giving this word in a particular manner.

Step Five

Write the word out in full and share it with leader(s). Take appropriate advice from the leadership.

Ꞔ What advice or counsel did your leaders give to you? Write out their thoughts to you here.

Ꞔ What are your own thoughts about what you are to do next? What would you change about the word you received? What additions would you make and what would you delete?

Building relationships with leadership is of prime importance to you and your relationship with the Holy Spirit. This is where we learn to demonstrate integrity and accountability.

Step Six

Make the adjustments and resubmit the prophecy to your advisor. Go through Step 5 again and further develop your case study.

Step Seven

When given the go-ahead to deliver the word, think about how you will do that. What method will you use?

☐ Written Word ☐ Symbolic Act ☐ Drama

☐ Spoken Word ☐ Visual Object ☐ Song

... or a combination of the above?

CS Explain on paper the method you will use and why. This helps you to focus and create the channel for the word to flow in your heart.

Step Eight

Choose the time and deliver the word. Make sure there is a leader or designated person present for accountability. You may want to have a tape recorder available to tape your blessing and encouragement.

Give yourself marks out of 10 (10 being the highest mark) for your actual delivery of the prophecy.

Marks out of 10	Your Mark	Leader's Mark
1. Conveying God's love and acceptance		
2. Introduction/putting people at ease		
3. Content of the prophecy		
4. Method of delivery/presentation		
5. Your own level of grace and humility		
6. Conclusion, prayer, and advice		

Describe what (if anything) you would change regarding points 1–6. What would you do differently? How would you improve things?

LEADERS ONLY: Please give your marks out of 10 in the space provided above and answer the following questions.

What do you think you could have been done better in points 1–6 above?

After reading the student's comments in the previous case study, do you agree with their perceptions? Please note here any comments you think would be helpful for their growth.

Step Nine

How was the prophecy recorded?

Were clarifications required at the conclusion of delivery? If so, what explanations were needed and why?

Finally! Describe how the workshop has affected your:

1. Perception of prophecy and how it should be used.

2. Working relationship with leaders.

3. Integrity and credibility in ministry.

4. Ability to feel and communicate God's heart to others.

Congratulations! If you have made it this far, you'll probably feel as if you've just completed your first competitive marathon. Hopefully you will have been stretched in mind and spirit. Now you need to practice and add experience in order for the whole process to become habitual and Godly.

Time allowed: 4–8 weeks

You will have learned how to:

1. Prepare your heart before the Lord, to listen carefully.

2. Pursue the love of God for your intended target people (1 Cor. 14:1a).

3. Decide the pattern and order of the word you are receiving.

4. Understand and explain the type of prophecy you have received.

5. Work with your leadership as you develop the prophecy.

6. Receive advice/counsel in the shaping of the prophecy.

7. Determine the methodology you will use in delivering the prophecy.

8. Examine honestly your practice of delivery and any adjustments you might make.

9. Administrate the prophecy correctly.

10. Submit to the feedback of your leadership/mentor.

11. Understand and express how the prophetic ministry has affected your personally.

12. Exercise self-control as you move from a purely spontaneous prophetic style to a more considered, planned, and disciplined prophetic approach to ministry.

Notes

Notes

Notes

Notes

FINAL APPLICATIONS

MODULE FOUR

Final Applications

WHAT YOU WILL FIND IN THIS SEGMENT:

- A meditation explanation and exercise
- A relational value and its application regarding non-negotiable love
- A life principle for prophetic ministry and its application regarding the nature of God
- A checklist for dialogue, discussion, and relationship building in partnership with leaders
- Development issues to safeguard the prophetic gift in the church in seeking help and support from leaders
- A prophetic word to be read, studied, and acted upon
- A recommended reading list

A MEDITATION AND EXPLANATION EXERCISE

To meditate means to think deeply about something or someone. It means to explore with mind and heart, allowing what you think to touch your innermost being.

Meditation is creative thought which leads us to the higher realm of revelation and wisdom. It takes us beyond the place of reason to where joy is seated and faith is activated.

Meditation allows us to search inside and outside the box of our current paradigm. What you see and hear there touches you profoundly. It adds a ring around the core truth of Christ, which is God within, the certainty of freedom.

Fruitful meditation is therefore not a casual seeking for revelatory insight. Initial creative thoughts are merely the "X" that marks the spot. There is treasure in meditation, a guarantee of wealth in the pursuit of God.

Many are satisfied with collecting random truth on the surface of their consciousness. It is good, wholesome stuff, but it does not satisfy and it cannot challenge the complexities of life in a warfare context.

Deep truth has to be mined over days and weeks. It takes joy and patience to take truth down to its deepest level. Beyond meeting our current needs. Beyond the depth of understanding the power it releases to us against our adversary. Down to the depth where God lives in the highest places of heaven. For all meditation must ultimately come before the throne of His majesty, sovereignty, and supremacy. He fills all things with Himself.

Our current situation requires wisdom, but even more it yearns for presence. Meditation allows us to experience both through the word coming alive in our spirit. Meditation leads us to God and the permission of His heart. Learn to be in the question peacefully with God. Let the Holy Spirit teach you how to abide. Turn inwardly and rest. Wait patiently. He will come. When your heart gets restless, turn to worship. When the interior atmosphere settles, return to listening.

Write down initial thoughts but do not pursue them just yet. Do not be distracted by what you hear initially. Set it aside and come back to it later.

When first entering a lifestyle of meditation, take care to ease into it slowly, an hour at first, then longer until half a day, and so on.

Always have a focus; do not try to wait in a vacuum. In this next exercise is a particular statement followed by a series of questions. This is both to give you practice in meditation and to bring you into revelation of God through the focus statement.

Use the questions as the Spirit leads. This exercise is not prescriptive but merely a guide to enable your contemplation. No doubt you will discover better questions as the Holy Spirit tutors you. Enjoy!

Meditation Exercise

> *"There are no good days and no bad days... only days of grace! Sometimes grace enables us to enjoy what is happening and other times grace gives us power to endure life's circumstances. Either way ... grace abounds and majesty comes into full view."*

- Engage your heart with the picture this statement provokes.
- What does this mean for you?
- What problems currently require more grace?
- What particular promise is the Holy Spirit drawing to your attention?
- Ask for scriptural support.
- Study the promise(s). Look for key words and phrases. Write down specifically what the Lord is guaranteeing to you in your current circumstances.
- How will you stand and position yourself before the Father?
- What level of confidence does the Father wish to bestow upon you?
- What fear, unbelief, and inadequacy must you give up in favor of the promise?
- Allow grace and majesty to come together in your heart. What picture of God's intentionality does it reveal to your current life circumstances?
- Now through the lens of that revelation, what has changed in your heart? Your viewpoint? Your mindset?
- Compose a prayer before the Lord, a request for His grace, kindness and power to enable you to receive.
- Write a psalm of thanksgiving to the Lord for what He has done in and for you in this current situation.
- Write out in full a confession and a declaration that you can speak into your circumstances by the power of the Holy Spirit.
- As you challenge your circumstances with your newfound revelation, a boldness and confidence will enter your speech. How did you feel?
- Continue declaring, believing, and challenging daily until God speaks further or your revelation takes hold of your heart.
- What has changed in you?
- What have you learned?
- What have you become in Christ?

- Finally, enter all these things in your journal. Keep a record of your walk with God in this way not only to encourage you in later times but to provide a legacy for your family and friends.

A Relational Value

- Do not merely treat this value as an exercise but as an opportunity to develop Christlike intent for yourself.
- Develop this value into a prophetic word in order to demonstrate the importance of your ministry arising out of your relationship with the Lord
- Read the Scriptures out loud several times.
- Think through the introductory paragraph and the main points.
- Work through Action Points 1–6 (see the following pages).
- Improve the Value Statement and make it your own.

Relationships of Openness and Honesty

Scriptures

Romans 12:9
Ephesians 4:15
Romans 2:1–11
2 Corinthians 4:1,2
Romans 6:12–14
2 Corinthians 7:1,2
1 John 1:5–10

A truly humble person does not fear being exposed. The great weakness in the western church is our refusal to accept that brokenness is a part of all life in the Spirit.

His power works best in weak people. Living in loving accountable relationships together enables us to walk in the light with God and give no place to the enemy.

Self-disclosure is vital to that process. A group of people who each know a part of our life and together know it all.

Discuss the following:

- Public and personal integrity through accountable friendships.
- It is the unshared areas of our life where Jesus is not Lord.
- Humility and honesty have the same root.
- Self-disclosure is a process involving definition.
- Humble people are small in their own eyes, honest about their struggles, and open to constructive criticism.
- Trust that you are loved, accepted, forgiven, and redeemed.

Action

To begin the process of self-disclosure and openness, start to look around and discover who, in friendship, may be trusted, over time, with certain parts of your life. Begin to develop a friendship with those people.

It takes time and love expressed and received before we can trust ourselves to self disclosure. The important thing is having a plan for friendship that includes accountability.

Value Statement

Relationships of openness and honesty allow us to drop the mask and the image we unconsciously present to the world. In this way we live in conscious freedom and joy before people as we do before God. Accepted in the Beloved, accepted in the body, accepted by self.

Action

1. Think of a situation in the past where you have not been open and honest about your life and lifestyle.
2. Take time to thoughtfully put together a letter to a loved one or a group of friends declaring your commitment to a more open and truthful way of living. Admit whatever fears or concerns you may have about this change in your life and request their help and support.
3. Using the relevant Scriptures in this exercise, put together a short teaching on Openness and Honesty as a way of life. Give it at a group meeting or to several of your friends.
4. Discuss the relevant points about how our friendships should represent God's holiness and goodness.
5. Pray together and over one another.
6. Practice, practice, practice!

A Life Principle for Prophetic Ministry

We must pursue our calling within a working structure of intentional relationships. This process will inevitably, some days, revolve around being purified, moving in loving confrontation, and experiencing the discipleship necessary to enable each one of us to grow up into all things in Christ. Cultivating values and principles in how we use our gifting will enable us to be proactive in our own development into a place of freedom and maturity.

We are all responsible for our own behavior. We are answerable to the Lord and to one another in the improvement and expansion of our gift and calling.

This life principle, if followed, will enable us to understand and experience the personality and character of the Lord Jesus as it relates to moving in the gift of prophecy.

Character With Charisma

In kingdom terminology, character is the basis of all success, not gifting. The Lord can add gifting to us in a single moment but character is made up of many hundreds of moments where decisions have to be made, often in difficult circumstances.

Our gifts and callings must continue to grow and develop in wisdom, power, and significance. At the same time our character is being tested and refined. We are learning to become more like Him. Character is not about perfection. Having integrity does not mean we never make mistakes, or do something stupid that we wish we could take back. It is about how we face these mistakes. It concerns how we open ourselves up for comment and input from significant others.

It is about our own levels of humility and accountability and how we pursue transformation of our whole nature before God. The Lord will process our character until it grows to the level of His dream for us. The caliber of our spirit will reveal our potential to reach the destiny that God has in mind for us. Grace is always hugely present when our quality is being rigorously tested.

Scriptures

1 Corinthians 12:4 to 13:3
Luke 16:9–14
Galatians 5:22, 23
1 Timothy 1:12–17
Titus 1:15 to 3:11
1 Timothy 4:6–16

With a group of friends or in your own quiet moments with the Lord, discuss the following:

1. Character is the private face and charisma the public one.
    a. How do we pursue a relationship with the Holy Spirit in both these areas, so that we maintain a healthy balance?

    b. How does our character work through our charisma?

2. Discuss the difference between our character and our personality.
    a. What do they each represent?

    b. How do we develop godliness in both?

3. We destroy our lack of character what we build through our gifting.
    a. What does walking in the light really mean?

    b. How do we develop relationships of mutual worth, trust, and value?

4. The degree to which we embrace our faults and problems is a measure of our character.
    a. When we are not truthful, lying takes the form of:
        - *Deleting* things that make us look bad.
        - *Distorting* what really happened and our part in it.
        - *Generalizing* about our words and actions that were not Christlike.

    b. Discuss what it means to tell the truth, the whole truth, and nothing but the truth.

    c. What would be different if Jesus were standing beside you?

Action

1. Pay attention to your character flaws. Seek accountability.

2. Help to support and mentor a friend in his or her search for a better quality of character. Learn to be gracious, firm and loving. Give and it shall be given to you.

3. At your funeral, what kind of statements would your friends say about your life and character? What would your associates at work say?

   a. Write your own eulogy — the things you would like to be said about you.

   b. What would have to change in you for that eulogy to be truthful?

   c. Talk to a friend about the kind of person you would like to become.

4. If you were to embrace humility, how different would your life be? How would it affect your relationships?

Value Statement

Being known is more important than knowing things. Character and charisma are inseparable. What matters is which has primacy.

What Kind of Partnership With Leaders?

1. Leaders want to see evidence that we are taking our gifting seriously, that we are pursuing the development and upgrade of our prophetic gifting.

2. We should be demonstrating that our methodology is changing in how we receive, work with, and deliver a prophetic word.

3. Leaders want to see interactive relationships with other people in a stronger team context, that we are serious about developing partnerships of real worth and value.

4. Leaders want prophetic people to understand the dynamics of authority, governing and leadership, and their place within those spheres of influence.

5. A stronger servant heart. Prophetic people having respect for others and gaining permission to speak through acts of service, display of character, and building good relationships.

6. Leaders want to see real evidence regarding the growth of people's relationship with the Lord. The Father trusts what He sees of the Son manifested in our lives.

7. Leaders want to see our commitment to personal growth and also corporate growth of the church and our part in that development.

8. When our lives are being tested, leaders want to see how we face adversity and warfare. This is where we learn to be trusted by others. What we learn and cultivate in our own times of crisis will be the bedrock of our support to enable others to breakthrough.

9. Leaders want to see our intimacy in worship and prayer. How we are cultivating our relationship with the Holy Spirit says a lot about us.

What Help and Support From Leaders?

1. Prophetic people need a secure place to fail. They need loving relationships that enable them to confront themselves regarding character, accountability, and gifting.

2. Everyone has fears. We all need an environment where we can be our real selves and get help to become more Christlike. We all need relationships of openness and honesty.

3. Prophetic people need godly examples of grace, mercy, and kindness. They need help to become New Testament prophets that work in line with the gospel of grace.

4. People need to develop from a purely spontaneous place of delivering prophecy to producing words that are crafted, prepared, and seasoned. They need more training that is specific and significant to their real issues and needs.

5. A continuous dialogue regarding where the church is now and where we are heading is essential. Times of prophetic praying about the present and future will create a stronger bond in vision and direction.

6. Prophetic people need key help and support to conquer their own fears, frustrations, and impatience. Often having a place to talk and share areas of difficulty is enough by itself. There are particular pressures on gifted people and they need a habitat that provides a context for loving adjustment.

A Prophecy

It is my intention to personalize My grace in such a way that you are empowered in specific areas of your life, so that rapid growth is the norm.

I give you favor so that you may know that you have special consideration for My intentional desire to take place, even in the ordinary things of life.

I am indulging Myself so that you will become highly confident, towards Me. Look at Me. Look at Me. Look at Me. I have given you permission to dream and to make request for specific issues, problems, situations, and circumstances.

Favor is now being actively promoted by the Holy Spirit and equally contested by the enemy. Favor is permission to ask, seek, knock in the sure and certain knowledge that God will say yes.

Your life therefore is about getting to "Yes"! I will take your favor into a high and deep place of confidence in My goodness so that a greater faith anointing begins to grow in you!

In this place of My indulgence I will teach you how to stand in the place of My desire. Your favor means you will stand in My presence and hear My heart saying yes.

I will teach you to make a new beginning in the place of My victory over the enemy of your soul!

I will develop in you the capacity to receive favor from people round about you. You will come to bask in My desire for you!

I will indulge Myself in your heart, your mind, and your life. My desires shall be made known and they shall become your dreams!

My will shall be revealed and you will walk in the awe of it, discovering the full majesty of My intent.

I am intentional says the Lord, I am intentional says the Lord, I am intentional says the Lord, and I will intensify My intentionality in your life until it takes hold of your own desires and dreams and you are transformed by My own delight!

My intentionality will become your identity and you will walk as Jesus walked — in the full knowledge and permission of the Father!

My indulgence creates a new identity in you and draws you out to a more powerful inheritance than you can possibly imagine.

In this place of My indulgent affection I will teach you the pleasurable discipline of working hand-in-hand with the Holy Spirit.

You will know who you are in Me for I shall declare and proclaim your identity joyfully!

Your faith will come to a new dynamic level of anointing to receive. I will push you into a deep place of receiving!!

I will joyfully position you in My manifest presence so that you will begin to occupy the territory of My heart and affection for you.

Final Applications

Come! Rest in My desire for you. Accept My benevolence. Depend on My desire to see you blessed.

The time of poverty is over: the place of fainting is behind you. Now you will see provision beyond imagining. Now you will see the goodness of the Lord in the land of the living.

Stand in this place. Recognize the place of your dreaming is also the place of your permission because I am indulging myself!

Adversity will come to unseat you from wild favor; warfare will contend with your promise. Neither will be able to remove you from the place of My continuous indulgence.

Come rest in My favor! Do not delay. I bestow upon you a newness of life and a spirit of wisdom and revelation that you would walk in agreement with Me.

It is an affair of the heart so you must think from the heart not the head. Do not be headstrong but be heartfelt. Lead from the heart and you will see the way, the provision, and the indulgence.

Behold, I mark the territory of your life with the claim pegs of victory. Each peg represents a desire of Mine for you to enjoy. Learn to live by My focus and My permissions.

I say yes and amen to you. I say yes and amen to you. I say yes and amen to you. I say yes and amen to you. You are a new creation living in a high place of My approval and My consent.

My indulgence is My gift to My beloved. You are My great love and I will deny you nothing that My great heart would willingly bestow.

Rise up My love and see yourself as My beloved. You are the one. You are the one. You are the one. I have set My heart on you. There is no rejection, only inclusion. Expect favor; expect My desire to be powerfully realized.

I will take your breath away. You will be astonished. You will marvel and be amazed. Expect favor. Be upgraded!

Change your current mindset. Learn a new language. Be trained to receive fullness. Measure no longer exists for you. Limitation has been cast aside.

All things are for your favor and to prove My desire for you. Refuse negativity. Begin to run. I will make you fit for life. I will give you the stamina required to run with a quickened spirit!

All your circumstances are now compatible with My desire. All situations are in agreement with My indulgence. So… ask and you will receive!

You are deeply, deeply loved and acceptable to Me. My heart is full toward you. Now you must take me at My word. My indulgence is knocking at the door of your heart.

Do not be governed by past failures and events. This is a new day. This is a new day. This is a new day. This is a new time. It is time to live a life overwhelmed. It is time to increase the speed of your response.

Say yes and come. Do not hang back or My heart can take no pleasure in you.

It is no risk to you if you come. There is only risk in the place of deliberation. If your head rules your heart you will be denied by your own caution.

Joy, thanksgiving, and rejoicing is the means by which you will both access and appropriate My desire.

This is not about you. This is not about you. This is not about you. It's My turn now. I will bless your name and make your name great and you will be a blessing!

Come up higher. Come to the place of your elevation. I lift you up. I lift you up.

My indulgence surrounds you as a shield. The Lord is your shepherd, you shall not want.

You are the seed of heaven and I plant you this night in the soil of My heartfelt indulgence. I will water your passion and everything that I have promised the Son shall come to you. I shall give you all you need to grow and be fruitful in My desire.

My indulgence is activated. It is released. It walks among you. Allow it to touch you, to shape your destiny, to develop your inheritance.

Do not say:

It is too much.

I am not good enough.

I cannot enter.

It's moving too fast.

You may enter by My permission not your performance. Look to Me and I will accelerate you. Make Me the Lord of your destination and I will get you there.

This is the same miracle as deliverance from Egypt… parting of the Red Sea… the provision of houses they did not build, vineyards they did not plant, and wells they did not dig… All these I did for Israel — shall I not do more for you who are in Christ?

Walk towards me asking. Walk towards me believing. Walk towards me seeing. Walk towards me receiving.

Behold, I challenge your believing. I provoke your heart to dream and desire. I stimulate your thinking to go to the place of risk and renewal.

I am coming after you. I am coming after you. I am coming after you. To woo you into a life unprecedented.

To court you, My beloved with passionate desire. Come away with Me to a new land of the Spirit where promises are the language of love between us.

This is the day of the Lord. Now is the accepted time. Your present and future has been decided and determined in My heart and permission.

Recommended Reading

Title	Author	Publisher
Hearing God	Dallas Willard	InterVarsity Press
The Gift of Prophecy	Jack Deere	Vine Books
Surprised by the Voice of God	Jack Deere	Zondervan
Growing in the Prophetic	Mike Bickle	Kingsway
The Seer	James Goll	Destiny Image
Prophetic Etiquette	Michael Sullivant	Creation House
The Prophets' Notebook	Barry Kissel	Kingsway
User Friendly Prophecy	Larry Randolph	Destiny Image
Prophecy in Practice	Jim Paul	Monarch Books
Can You Hear Me?: Tuning in to the God Who Speaks	Brad Jersak	Trafford Press
When Heaven Invades Earth	Bill Johnson	Treasure House
Knowledge of the Holy	A. W. Tozer	O. M. Publishing
The Pleasures of Loving God	Mike Bickle	Creation House
Manifest Presence	Jack Hayford	Chosen
Living the Spirit-Formed Life	Jack Hayford	Regal
The Agape Road	Bob Mumford	Lifechangers
The Sensitivity of the Spirit	R. T. Kendall	Hodder & Stroughton
Living in the Freedom of the Spirit	Tom Marshall	Sovereign World
Secrets of the Secret Place	Bob Sorge	Oasis House
The Heart of Worship	Matt Redman	Regal
Experiencing the Depths of Jesus Christ	Jeanne Guyon	Seedsowers
The Unsurrendered Soul	Liberty Savard	Bridge-Logos

About the Prophetic Equipping Series

Graham began teaching prophetic schools in 1986. Eight years later he wrote *Developing Your Prophetic Gifting,* a book which has won universal acclaim. Translated into numerous languages, reprinted many times over and published by several companies, it has been a best seller and widely regarded as a classic. Graham has continued to develop new material each year in the Schools of Prophecy. Now after almost twenty years of teaching continuously upgrading material, the School of Prophecy has developed into one of the finest teaching programs on the prophetic gift, ministry and office of a Prophet. This new material effectively makes *Developing Your Prophetic Gifting* redundant.

The Prophetic Equipping Series encompasses six volumes that combine classic teaching with the journal format so popular in the *Being with God Series.* It also embraces a workshop and training manual, with emphasis on producing one of the finest teaching aids on the prophetic gift and ministry. These manuals are appropriate for individual, small group or church-wide use. All Christians can prophesy and would benefit from Graham's wisdom and experience in ministry. The assignments, exercises, workshops, lectio divina and other material are designed to further the understanding of the prophetic gift, ministry and office. If used properly, the process will develop accountability for prophetic people, healthy pasturing of the prophetic, and give relevant questions for leadership and prophetic people to ask one another. The series includes:

Volume 1 – Approaching the Heart of Prophecy
Volume 2 – Prophecy & Responsibility
Volume 3 – Prophetic Wisdom
Volume 4 – The Prophetic Impact
Volume 5 – Prophetic Partnerships
Volume 6 – Prophecy and the Ways of God

To find more information on Graham's training schools and events, please visit www.GrahamCooke.com

About the Author

Graham Cooke is part of The Mission's core leadership team, working with senior team leader, David Crone, in Vacaville, California. Graham's role includes training, consulting, mentoring and being part of a think tank that examines the journey from present to future.

He is married to Theresa, who has a passion for worship and dance. She loves to be involved in intercession, warfare, and setting people free. She cares about injustice and abuse, and has compassion on people who are sick, suffering and disenfranchised.

They have six children and two grandchildren. Ben and Seth both reside and work in the UK. Ben is developing as a writer, is very funny, and probably knows every movie ever made. Seth is a musician, a deep thinker with a caring outlook and an amazing capacity for mischief.

Sophie and her husband Mark live in Vacaville and attend The Mission. Sophie & Mark are the Operations Managers of Brilliant Book House, the publishing company of Graham Cooke. Sophie has played a significant part in Graham's ministry for a number of years, and has helped develop resources, new books and journals, as well as organize events. Mark and Sophie are a warm-hearted, friendly, deeply humorous couple with lots of friends. Mark and Sophie have three daughters. Evelyn (August 2006) is a delight; a happy little soul who likes music, loves to dance and enjoys books. Annabelle (December 2008) is lovely, happy, content and very tiny. Penelope Violet joined us in February 2011 and is adored by her sisters — and all the rest of us!

Their other daughters are Alexis, who is loving, kind and gentle, and very intuitive and steadfast toward her friends; and Alyssa, a very focused and determined young woman who is fun-loving with a witty sense of humor.

Also, Graham and Theresa have two beautiful young women, Julianne and Megan, both in Australia, who are a part of their extended family.

Graham is a popular conference speaker and is well known for his training programs on the prophetic, spiritual warfare, intimacy and devotional life, leadership, spirituality and the church in transition. He functions as a consultant and freethinker to businesses, churches, and organizations, enabling them to develop strategically. He has a passion to establish the Kingdom and build prototype churches that can fully reach a post-modern society.

A strong part of Graham's ministry is in producing finances and resources to the poor and disenfranchised in developing countries. He supports many projects specifically for widows, orphans and people in the penal system. He hates abuse of women and works actively against human trafficking and the sex slave trade, including women caught up in prostitution and pornography.

If you would like to invite Graham to minister or speak at an event, please complete the online Ministry Invitation Form at www.GrahamCooke.com.

If you wish to become a financial partner for the sake of missions and compassionate acts across the nations, please contact his office at office@myemerginglight.com, and his administrative assistant will be happy to assist you.

You may contact Graham by writing to:

Graham Cooke
865 Cotting Ln, Ste C
Vacaville, California
95688, USA

www.GrahamCooke.com

Welcome to

Reaching Christians For Christ

Graham Cooke is an acclaimed author who started writing twenty years ago, releasing his first book in 1990 and selling over 400,000 copies worldwide. Graham has since rewritten this material into a new edition called *The Prophetic Equipping Series,* which will be six volumes. Volumes 1–3 are available now. These are *Approaching the Heart of Prophecy, Prophecy & Responsibility* and *Prophetic Wisdom.*

Download Graham's e-books **today!**

All of Graham's books and interactive journals are available to download directly onto your computer, eliminating shipping costs!

Graham has written over 14 titles, on subjects ranging from how to craft a prayer, understanding what is really going on in the spirit when God seems to be distant and when He is drawing close, understanding God's nature and many others.

Brilliant boasts an extensive collection of Graham's work. We distribute his CDs, MP3s, DVDs, books and Interactive Journals and offer a direct link between Graham and our customers through our newsletters, YouTube channel and podcasts.

Search for "Graham Cooke" on Facebook and be the first to receive updates on new projects, events and resources.

"At Brilliant Book House, we believe you have a unique call on your life that can only be found in God. He has something for you that is far beyond your wildest dreams. As you step out into that purpose, we want to stand with you, offering you encouragement, training and hope for your journey. We want to equip you for what God wants to do in you, and through you. That is our promise to you."

–Graham Cooke

Brilliant Book House is a California-based publishing company founded and directed by Graham Cooke and is dedicated to producing high-quality Christian resources and teaching materials. Our vision is to equip all of our readers to lead brilliant lives, confidently led by the Holy Spirit into the destiny God has for them.

Brilliant has a passion for the Kingdom of Heaven, a powerful desire to see the Body of Christ comes into full dynamic stature in the earth, and a hunger for everyone in Jesus to discover their rightful places in the purposes of God.

The world needs to see God in a ***brilliant*** way.

Visit us online today:

www.BrilliantBookHouse.com